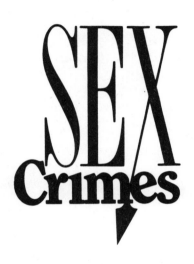

DEDICATION

Jayme

Kellye

Christian

Ronald M.
HOLMES

SEX
Crimes

SAGE PUBLICATIONS
The International Professional Publishers
Newbury Park   London   New Delhi

For information address:

SAGE Publications, Inc.
2455 Teller Road
Newbury Park, California 91320
E-mail: order@sagepub.com

SAGE Publications Ltd.
6 Bonhill Street
London EC2A 4PU
United Kingdom

SAGE Publications India Pvt. Ltd.
M-32 Market
Greater Kailash I
New Delhi 110 048 India

Printed in the United States of America

Library of Congress Cataloging-in-Publication Data

Holmes, Ronald M.
  Sex crimes / Ronald M. Holmes
      p.   cm.
  ISBN 0-8039-3952-3. — ISBN 0-8039-3953-1 (pbk.)
  1. Sex crimes—United States.   2. Sex offenders—United States.
I. Title.
HQ72.U53H638   1991
364.1'53—dc20
                                                                90-19480
                                                                    CIP

97 98 99 00 01 14 13 12 11 10 9

Contents

Preface and Acknowledgments

There are few topics that capture the attention and imagination of Americans more than sex crime and the sex criminal. Crimes such as rape, lust murder, and child molestation appall and disgust, as well as fascinate, most Americans. Serial killers, anthropophagists, triolists, rapists, and frotteurs all galvanize the concern of those who are victimized and those who experience their actions secondhand, through the media.

In lecturing throughout the United States on sex crimes, psychological profiling, and satanic and ritualistic crimes, I am constantly being told stories about the sex acts and habits of people who mainly come into contact with the criminal justice system in general and the police in particular. Realizing there is a dearth of information regarding the wide variety of sex crimes and sex criminals, I set about gathering information about sexual attitudes and behaviors, and sex offenders and their offenses. In gathering information for this text, I researched books, articles, and case studies. I also conducted personal interviews and carried out written correspondence with several infamous persons; Ted Bundy, Doug Clark, John Gacy, Wayne Williams, and others either spoke or wrote to me about violence while typically maintaining their own innocence. Regardless of these men's crimes, each has his own point of view. One in particular (not mentioned by name) provided a great deal of information, especially concerning fantasy and sadism. Caught in a web of violent fantasies, he carried out many cruel sexual attacks on women and children. In prison for the rest of his life, this man has given me more information about what happens in the mind of a sex criminal than all of the reading I have done in my years of research.

Of course, there are many others to whom I owe a debt of gratitude. In no particular order, I would like to list a few: Dr. Al Carlisle, Utah State Prison; Sgt. David Rivers, Dade County Sheriff's Office; Lt. Jeff Moody, Louisville (Kentucky) Police Department; Capt. Ralph Hernandez, Broward County Sheriff's Office; James Massie, Kentucky Probation and Parole Office; Anne Rule, author; Sgt. George Barret, Louisville Police Department; Bob Crouse, seminar manager for the Southern Police Institute; Joyce Wilson, Louisville Rape Relief Center; Maj. Edward Mercer, Louisville Police Department; Det. Walt Parsons, Arvada (Colorado) Police Department; Chief of Police Jerry Beavers, Asheville (North Carolina) Police Department; Dr. George Nichols, chief medical examiner for the Commonwealth of Kentucky; Dr. R. F. Greathouse, coroner, Jefferson County, Kentucky; Dr. Edward Latessa, University of Cincinnati; Dr. Larry Gaines, Eastern Kentucky University; Norman Pomrenke, past director of the Southern Police Institute; Dr. Gary Sykes, director of the Southwest Police Training Center; Father Jacobson, Oregon State Penitentiary; and Blaise Donnelly, Sage Publications.

I would particularly like to thank my wife, Tootie. She still shakes her head at my research and writing efforts. My sons, Craig, Steve, and Terry, deserve some attention because of the remarks made to them about their dad's work. I thank them all. They are the important people in my life.

Ronald M. Holmes

1

Sex Crimes in the United States: A Brief Overview

During an interview the year before he was executed, serial murderer Ted Bundy told me the following story. The killer of 12-year-old Kimberly Leach had a rich fantasy life. "He [the unknown killer, Ted said] entered her vaginally from the rear, pulled her head back by the hair and slit her throat. The most powerful orgasm this person ever had" (author's files). Refusing at the time to admit any culpability for any crime, Bundy stated that he had been around enough criminals to have an understanding of their fantasies and actions.

These statements reveal a personality that has made a vital connection between sexual pleasure and violent aggression. In no society can such actions be deemed either permissible or desirable. The taking of another person's life or the deprivation of another's liberty in pursuit of one's own pleasure is not tolerable in a civilized society. However, not all sexual aggression takes such extreme form.

Sex has been with society forever, and the purpose of sex as well as the roles of men and women have changed over the years. That humans primarily

TABLE 1.1.   Standards of Sexual Behavior

Standard	*Description*
Statistical	what most people do
Religious	what one's religion permits or prohibits
Cultural	what one's culture encourgages or discourages
Subjective	persons judge their own behavior

"copulate to populate" is no longer true. Now, it appears that many people "copulate to recreate."

WHAT IS NORMAL SEX?

To answer such a question is to open a Pandora's box. What is normal to one person may be very bizarre to the next. Individual differences notwithstanding, however, there are standards in any society that determine acceptable behavior.

All societies regulate the behavior, including the sexual behavior, of their members. There are some sexual behaviors that many societies find totally unacceptable, deeming them repugnant. For example, in the United States, incest is against the law in every state. This does not mean, however, that everyone abides by the same set of laws and standards.

SEXUAL STANDARDS

There are at least four standards used to determine "normalcy" (see Table 1.1). Of course, not everyone agrees on which standard is the most important or is applicable in a particular case. The decision to cite a norm depends not only on the person but also on the general and particular circumstances.

Statistical Standard

If more than half the people in a sample commit or perform some act, this norm could validate normalcy for that group of people. For example, it may be that in the United States today more than 50% of all once-married persons have ended a marriage in divorce. Is it normal to be divorced? If one uses only the statistical standard, then it is indeed normal. Another example: If more than 50% of males masturbate, then is masturbation normal?

Using only the statistical standard can be dangerous, because it can make lawbreaking appear "normal." For instance, many teenage girls shoplift makeup or items of jewelry—perhaps even the majority do so. Does this make it normal to steal?

Cultural Standard

In every society there are cultural rules, including sets of words, ideas, customs, and beliefs that govern that society. For instance, in American society, it is against the law for a person to have more than one spouse at a time. The Mormon church in the nineteenth century took its case to the U.S. Supreme Court, hoping the Court would allow Mormons to practice polygyny as a basic tenet of their faith, but the Supreme Court rejected the claim. Our society does allow serial monogamy (i.e., multiple marriages, but one at a time), but not polygamy.

Culture is the normative structure of a society. There can be no society without rules; there can be no society without culture. Our culture attempts to regulate, in some fashion, sexual behavior. Pedophilia, incest, rape, lust murder, exhibitionism, and other sexually aberrant behaviors are viewed negatively by the majority of American citizens. In addition to opposition to these forms of sexual patterns and behavior, there are rules and admonitions against those who practice them. This is not to say that all people agree on these standards. Members of the North American Man/Boy Love Association would not agree. Another pedophile organization, the Rene Guyon Society, has a motto, "Sex Before Eight or It's Too Late." This is hardly a position with which most would agree.

Religious Standard

Historically, religion has played an important role in the development of the value systems of countries and individuals. Only a few years ago, many Christians were guided by strong and absolute guidelines. Certain acts constituted grievous sins. If one committed those acts, some of which were sexual in nature, one was assured of inevitable punishment, possibly eternal damnation, if true contrition was not shown.

There are conspicuous differences that develop from statistical, cultural, and religious standards when they interact with each other. For example, to use again the example of divorce, more than 50% of once-married people are divorced and wish to remarry. Most do. Also, our society readily admits those who have remarried back into the fold of "acceptable persons"; they are not stigmatized as in years past. However, there are some religious persons who believe that one is married "till death do us part," and neither divorce nor remarriage is a possibility.

Religion plays a very important role in many persons' lives. It determines the rightness or wrongness of their behavior. In matters of sex, it may play a pivotal role, as it determines the acceptability of certain sex acts.

Subjective Standard

This is perhaps the most important standard in any person's life. This standard legitimates behavior in the same fashion as statistical, cultural, and religious standards, but at the personal level. For instance, take the last time you drove slightly above the speed limit on an interstate highway. Chances are there were many drivers passing you as you drove along. Even though you were violating the speed limit, others were doing the same thing, and you may have rationalized your lawbreaking, saying, "They were driving much faster than I was."

Talking with students in classes at the University of Louisville, a question I often ask is, "When was the last time you stole something?" Many students will admit that the pens they are taking notes with were stolen. If a pen came from the student's workplace, the story quickly follows that the boss was a jerk, the student was not paid enough for the work he or she was doing, the employer would never miss the pen because there were so many other pens, or whatever. A multitude of subjective rationalizations can be offered for the act of thievery, an act of deviance.

Even rape can be legitimated. Susan Brownmiller (1975) states that rape has historically been viewed as permissible in terms of a victorious army further victimizing the vanquished by raping the women of the conquered. The soldier who rapes a village woman would not view this as a criminal and sexual act, but as something he deserves as a "conquering hero." Moreover, there are more than a few states where a husband cannot be criminally charged with the rape of his wife.

But it is not enough simply to legitimize the acts that may be judged deviant by some other members of the society; we must feel that what we are doing is not only normal, but "really not that bad." This last standard is the most important.

ELEMENTS IN SEXUAL BEHAVIOR

When I first started lecturing to police audiences throughout the United States, I informed my students that there were four elements in deviant sex. But I had a real problem—I found that these four elements also existed within my own sexual value system. I was forced to reexamine my personal values; either I was a sex offender or these four elements were quite normal. I prefer to think of myself as "normal" (whatever that is), and others I considered to be normal also possessed the same elements. What, then, separated sex offenders who possess the elements from those who are not adjudicated sex offenders? This is a question that is quite difficult to address fully.

Fantasy

To be sexual, one must have a sexual fantasy. It is impossible to be sexual without one. It is true that often when males are raped, they will experience erection, but this erection is more hormonally connected with fear than with sexual arousal. It also is true that a woman may experience coitus without becoming sexually aroused. However, in neither case can the person be said to be "sexual." Each is a passive actor in a sexual act—one a violent act where sex is the weapon used, and one a sexual act performed when the mind is elsewhere occupied. But to be sexually involved, either with another person or in an autoerotic circumstance, fantasy is an absolute necessity.

Some fantasies are quite rich in content, some are exceedingly simple, and others may be quite bizarre and lie in the realm of the "abnormal." Take, for example, the following fantasy related to me by a pedophile. Having an interest in 12-year-old girls, he fantasized about the kidnapping, rape, and finally the murder and cannibalism of young girls.

Following an earthquake, two 16-year-old boys were exploring a cemetery near their own home. Noticing a hole in the ground where there had not been one before, the boys decided to explore. They discovered a cave, and their eyes slowly became acclimated to the darkness. Looking at one wall, they saw a skeleton chained to the wall. At the foot of the skeleton was clothing that belonged to the victim, an apparent 11- or 12-year-old female. Looking around the cave, they discovered another skeleton chained to the opposite wall. Again, clothing was at the foot of this skeleton. Frightened, the two boys started to flee the cave.

As the boys were climbing out of the cave, an adult blocked their leaving, and in a loud voice demanded to know what the boys were doing in the cave. Effectively intimidating the boys, the adult instructed the boys to fetch him a 12-year-old girl for his pleasure. The two boys went to a local drugstore and awaited a young girl venturing outside the store. Abducting the first one they could get, they took her back to the cave. The two boys were instructed by the adult to rape and sodomize the young victim while he watched. After repeatedly abusing the young girl, they chained her to a wall, the same wall where they had already taken down the skeleton.

Repeating this abuse for several days, the man demanded that the two boys go back to the drugstore for another girl. They abducted a second girl, and the victim was taken to the cave, where she was raped as the first young girl was forced to watch.

After several days, the first girl said she was hungry. Building a fire, the second victim was torn apart and her arms and legs were roasted over a fire. The chained victim was forced to eat the roasted parts of the second victim. Immediately after, the first young victim was strangled to death.

The parting remark made by the man was, "You two boys meet me here tomorrow. I need two more young bitches!" (author's files)

Such is the fantasy of an aggressive and sadistic child offender, a mysoped. Most persons do not share the aggressive component that is an integral part of this pedophile's fantasy. But everyone does indeed have sexual fantasies. Most people's fantasies center on willing partners in consensual, "normal" sexual acts.

Symbolism

Sex is very visual. Sex sells. Look at the manner in which sex is used to sell automobiles, beer, and even household appliances. When one speaks of sexual symbolism, fetishisms and partialisms are evident. A fetish is an inanimate object to which sexual feelings have been attached. It appears that every male has at least one sexual fetish. Bras, panties, garter belts, and negligees are all common fetishes. There are more unusual fetishes also. One rapist I interviewed stated that he was erotically aroused whenever he climbed through a window to burglarize a home. He made certain that when he broke into a home the man of the house was not there. In climbing through the window, he would experience an erection and then an orgasm. Since he believed it was abnormal to experience an orgasm in this fashion, he fantasized that he should rape the female in the home. Raping a woman was normal; experiencing an orgasm climbing through a window was abnormal.

A partialism is an isolated part of the body to which sexual feelings have been attached. Breasts, legs, and buttocks are good examples of partialisms in our society. Both men and women have partialisms. Ted Bundy was supposed to be attracted to women with long dark hair that was parted in the middle (although many of his victims did not fit that mold).

Ritualism

Sex offenders are ritualistic, but this same statement may be made of others who are sexually active. For example, married couples who have been together for years almost "intuitively" know when their partners are sexually receptive—the manner in which certain words are spoken or certain gestures are made, or the ways a myriad of other words or deeds are committed or omitted, can carry sexual messages.

With many sex offenders, however, the element of ritualism is one that has increased almost to the point of addiction. One serial sex offender stated that when he was 9 years old he read a book of pornography that depicted a sadistic rape. Nine years later, as a college freshman, he raped his first victim. He forced her to say the words that were spoken by the raped female in the story he read as a child. With each subsequent rape, he forced the victim to repeat the same words and sentences that he had learned as a child.

In ritualism, the sexual acts have to be performed in the same fashion and often in the same sequence. If not done as "the script provides," the act has to be either abandoned or restarted. Some rapists, for example, may force their victims to repeat certain phrases or even to call them by different names. This may become very important when investigators question the victims. The first name used by a rapist may be his mother's or wife's name.

Compulsion

"I woke up one morning knowing I was going to kill, like I had woken up many mornings before," one serial sadistic sex offender told me. "It is an awful, gnawing feeling deep down in my stomach which impels me to rape and kill," he continued.

"There is something deep inside of me, something I can't control. . . . It's so strong." So said Ted Bundy to Don Patchen when being interrogated in Pensacola, Florida, in 1978. "There's something wrong with me," he continued. "I don't give a shit about those people" (D. Patchen, personal communication, November 1986). These compulsive feelings well up inside the serial sex offender and launch him into action.

The longer the period between the sexual acts, the more the acts take on a different character. For example, when Ted Bundy killed at the Chi Omega sorority house at Florida State University, he had not killed for more than two years. The character of his killings there was much different from that of his killings out West or the killing that followed only three weeks later.

A rapist who was attracted to young girls told me that when he was feeling the need to rape he drove to a corner where he had picked up several women in the past. He waited for his choice of victim, a "slender, cheerleader type," but he could find no one who fit his *ideal victim type*. Then he saw two 12-year-old girls walking across a field, and since he was feeling the need to kill and the feeling was so strong, he abducted and sexually abused both.

COMBINING THE ELEMENTS

It is true that all "normally sexually active persons" have the four elements described above. What accounts for these elements in perverse sexual activity? This is a difficult question to address properly. The following scenarios are certainly indicative that the sex involved is not typical of "normal" sexual functioning: when an individual is sexual only when a certain fetish or partialism is present; when compulsivity is so overwhelmingly potent that emotions and caring for the partner are missing; when certain scripts must be followed, and any deviation from them is fatal to sexual functioning; and when fantasies center on the dehumanization, torture, and murder of hapless and helpless victims.

2

Sex and History

To understand the role and practice of sexual behavior, it is necessary to view it in historical perspective. One way to do this is to analyze certain family types as they existed throughout the ages and their modal viewpoints regarding sex and sexuality. This is the approach that will be taken in this chapter. Several types of families—ancient Jewish, Greek, Roman, and Christian—will be examined, along with their historical periods, to provide some perspective on today's views on sexual activity, both "normal" sex and socially judged criminal sex offenses.

FAMILY TYPES

The Hebrew Family

Several centuries before the time of Christ, the ancient Jewish family had characteristics that grew out of necessity, because of Jews' status in the world. They were a small group of people, nomadic because of circumstance, and, because of their religious beliefs and practices, persecuted by various captor peoples. The Jewish family had four main characteristics: It was patriarchal, patrilineal, patrilocal, and polygynous.

Regarding the element of patriarchy, it must be said that in the ancient Hebrew family, the father was indeed the supreme commander. His word was law; he was the rabbi, the judge, the jury, and—in perhaps more than a few cases—the executioner. Bloodlines were traced through the father's side of the family.

Males, both adults and children, were granted higher status because of their sex. The desired children were male because sons had certain abilities that were judged to be superior to those of daughters—they were stronger, able to do heavier work, and could act as warriors in battle. All monies and properties typically were passed down from the father to the eldest son (the eldest legitimate son, if there was one). The eldest married son also lived close to the father's home (this is the patrilocal trait). This son, the heir, would inherit not only his father's privileges, wealth, and property, but his father's responsibilities as well.

Of course, in some cases, wives were unable to beget children. Consider the case of Sarah and Abraham in the Old Testament. Barren, Sarah had not been able to give Abraham the son he so desperately desired. She encouraged him to seek a concubine who would bear him a son. Abraham chose Hagar, and from this union came a son, Ishmael. Later, Sarah herself bore Abraham his second son, Isaac. Although Ishmael had held the preferred position of first born, Isaac was legitimate, so Ishmael was forced to relinquish his special status to Isaac.

Of course, divorce was not permitted to the women in the Jewish family. The male was granted divorce and was also permitted to have multiple wives. This practice, polygyny (one husband with two or more wives), is suited for a family system where there are not enough men for all the women or when a drastic increase in the population is desirable. As stated earlier, this was a small, persecuted group of people, and they needed sons to act as warriors. God had no commandment against the practice of polygyny among these people. Indeed, it was thought that everyone should marry, especially men. But one had to be careful not to commit adultery or fornication.

Again, consider the case of Samson. There was nothing especially sinful about Samson's sexual liaison with Delilah in and of itself. God became angry with Samson because of the position that Delilah held in Babylonian society. Delilah was a priestess of Ishtar, a female fertility goddess of the cult of Marduk. By having sexual intercourse with Delilah, Samson was worshiping a false god, Marduk. This was the sin of Samson, not telling Delilah that the secret of his strength was in his hair.

Sex in the Hebrew family was primarily reserved for procreation and for the pleasure of the male. Women were not to enjoy sex because it was their "pleasure" to raise the children and take care of the home.

The Greek Family

Before the time of Christ, the ancient Greek family took a practical approach to the subject of sex. The purposes of heterosexual sex were seen to be procreation and, of course, affection. But the highest form of love affair was considered to be that between two males, one an adult and the other a young boy before puberty. Homosexuality was "institutionalized" in Greek society.

The status of the woman was low in the Greek family. The married woman had principally only two roles: wife and mother. Her education was restricted to that required for her to run a household and fulfill the needs of motherhood. If a man wanted to have an adult conversation with a woman about civics, astronomy, government, or philosophy, it was difficult, for there were only a few women educated in these areas. One educated group of women were the hetaerae, prostitutes who were educated not only formally but also in ways to please their male customers. Indeed, married women were seldom seen in the public company of their husbands.

The Greek male was allowed to obtain a divorce, something that was extremely difficult, and in most cases impossible, for the ordinary woman. This family type was also male dominated; sons were needed to carry on the family name, inherit family wealth, and act as warriors.

Sex in ancient Greece was not only procreational but recreational. Homosexuality, lesbianism, hedonism, polytheism, and a warlike and monogamous family structure were all traits that typified the ancient Greek family.

The Roman Family

Like the Greek family, the Roman family was patriarchal, patrilineal, patrilocal, and monogamous. However, this family type was very important as far as the sexual beliefs of the families that were to follow were concerned, because the Roman family was the first family type that allowed equal status for males and females. Belief in equal status for the sexes led to the concept of bihumanity—what was good for one sex was equally good for the other. Thus the world of the private life, the home and family, was just as important as the world of the public sphere. Just because one was different from the other did not make one more important than the other.

There were other important differences in this family. It was true, for example, that males were desired as children. They would act as warriors, inherit the family wealth, and carry on the family name. But daughters were also desired. They could accumulate property and even serve as elected officials in government. They could also sue for divorce. The concept of hedonism became firmly implanted in the societal fabric—live for today because one does not know what tomorrow brings.

Many of the various rituals found in wedding ceremonies today come from this family. The parade through town, the wedding ring, and the carrying of the spouse across the threshold all date back to the Roman family before the time of Christ. It is true that the father was still in control of the family, but the mother was now treated as an equal.

The sexual values of the family included not only sex as procreation but also sex as recreation. Sex was something that was viewed as a normal part of a personality and was to be enjoyed. There was nothing wrong with sex. Neither homosexual nor heterosexual sex was sinful. Roman religion was predicated upon plural gods, and these gods were not totally bent on vengeance and war. There were gods of emotion and pleasure as well; when an individual became intoxicated it was sometimes viewed as though he or she had received special visitation from the gods.

From all of the special traits of the Roman family, the Christian family arose. But because early Christians were a small group of people, persecuted and reviled, it was only natural that they would overturn and replace many of the social and sexual values that the Romans held dear.

The Christian Family

After years of persecution, the Christian family gained power and recognition in Rome. Prescribing values that were foreign to the traditional Roman family, the Christians went about overturning the values that were indigenous to the Romans.

Unlike the other three family types that have been discussed, the Christians believed that it was better to remain single, but if you could not contain yourself, it was better to marry than to burn (I Corinthians 7:9). As St. Paul stated, "It is better that you remain as I" (that is, single). Of course, Jesus never uttered such words as these, but he may have set an example of his erotic-phobic posture when he doctrinally refused to be born of a natural sexual union between a husband and a wife and also when he was not married, at least in his public life. There are more than a few theologians who believe that Christ may indeed have been married, because there was a severe Roman tax placed upon single males once they reached a certain age. This tax almost ensured that every man would marry, because the average man at that time would have found it very difficult to pay the tax.

The Christian family incorporated many of the same traits as the earlier family types. It insisted, for example, on monogamy (if a man could not control himself he thus had to marry), but did not allow for divorce. The purest men did not marry at all, but instead dedicated all their efforts to the work of preparing for the next world.

Sex was considered utilitarian; it was not to be used for recreation, as was the practice of the Romans. Sex was for procreation and not for pleasure. After all, Mary, the mother of Jesus, was a virgin and did not involve herself in a conjugal fashion with her husband, Joseph. She was mystically impregnated by the Holy Spirit, and Joseph had nothing to do with this pregnancy. Moreover, Mary was free from the stain of Original Sin, a Christian dogma that was not made an integral part of the belief of the Church until several hundred years later.

It does not appear that Jesus was as firmly opposed to the joys of sex as were many of his followers. Take, for example, St. Simon the Stylite. A hermit, he lived in a cave in the desert for years without bathing. He wore a rope around his waist, which became infected with maggots, and as the maggots fell from his festering wounds upon the floor of the cave, his famous prayer was, "Eat little children what God has given unto you." St. Perpetua, an early Church martyr, made a vow of virginity when she was 7 years old. At 12 she married, and on the wedding night, her husband "demanded the marriage debt" (sexual intercourse). She refused, citing her vow of years past. Her husband gave her time to reconsider this vow, with the admonition that unless she relented, he would have four horses pull her body apart the next morning. She remained adamant, as did her husband, and she indeed was killed the next morning. Other examples are not as dramatic. St. Silvia, a virgin, refused to bathe. She washed only her fingertips for more than 60 years. It is not difficult to understand why there were so many virgins at this time.

The status of women fell drastically during this time. Women, after all, were considered to be the source of all evil. If it were not for Eve, Adam would not have sinned. She led him to the devil's temptation and enticed him into sin. The concept of women as evil took deep root at this time; some early church fathers became so entrenched in their values regarding the inferior position of women that one theologian even stated that he believed that women were nothing but phlegm and bad blood. But women were needed despite all of their supposed bad characteristics, for women begat children.

And in spite of negative attitudes toward women, and in contrast to the desire of the other early family types for male children, the Christians wanted daughters because they stood a better chance of remaining virginal.

THE FAMILY IN THE MIDDLE AGES

As the family moved into the Middle Ages, the Church seized control, and the Church has still not changed to any great extent regarding attitudes and values concerning sex. The Church ecclesiastically mandated a list of sins that proscribed certain sexual acts that the Church believed were against natural law as well as Church law. For example, masturbation was considered to be a sin punishable by a year of penance. Subsequent acts of masturbation resulted in longer periods of penance outside the church, confessing this sin to passers-by, and collecting alms for the Church. Women were considered to be sinners if they loitered around the church building after midnight. There were sanctions against having sex with one's spouse on holy days and for 40 days before and after Easter, and against acts of homosexuality. Obviously, birth control and abortion were viewed as abominations, because neither would lead to population increase, thus violating the sole purpose of marital sex.

Sex had now become intimately connected with procreation. Women's status was again low, despite the age of chivalry. The carnal nature of man was satisfied by the wife, a carnal creature indeed. The pure love relationship was never consummated or tainted by sex. True love was an idealized, platonic arrangement, a love that was often never confronted by a personal or intimate relationship.

Under the ever-watchful eye of the Church, sex was utilitarian—its sole purpose was procreation. This position was so firm that the Church went so far as to consider it sinful for a husband and wife to have sexual intercourse once the wife passed childbearing age.

CURRENT SEXUAL STANDARDS

Attitudes toward sex and sexuality have changed drastically since the time of the early Jewish family. In the early history of the United States, sex was still viewed as a method of propagation of the species. At the turn of the twentieth century the status of women was still low. Women were beginning to elevate their own status, fighting for their own rights—the right to vote, for example—and as the society moved into the mid-twentieth century, women were demanding equal rights in all spheres of their lives, including their sexual lives.

The old double standard began to crumble in the twentieth century, but there is no doubt that remnants of this standard are still with us today. There are still many who believe that it is permissible for men to "sow some wild oats" but who would deny this same behavior to women. Where did we get this idea and value? Such values and attitudes have been passed down from one generation to the next, with each generation accepting, changing, and adding to them in different ways. What is needed at a particular time by one generation influences what is deemed important and vital to the existence of the society.

Consider the current relatively liberal attitudes toward homosexuality, birth control, and abortion. All three of these practices represent some form of population control. If, because of some natural or human-made catastrophe, society suddenly needed a great increase in the number of children born, it is reasonable to expect that there would be a change in society's values and attitudes toward these practices.

The sexual standards that are apparent in today's society reflect the needs of society. The traditional repressive asceticism of early family forms is no longer a mainstream sexual standard. Sex only for the male and solely for procreation is not a viable standard for members of today's society. We have also moved away, as a society, from restricting sexual expression only to those persons who are married.

The modal sexual expression appears to be sex with love or strong affection. This is coupled also with a sense of strong commitment and maybe even a plan for marriage. Of course, there are some who believe that love or strong affection is really not needed for sex to occur; swingers (mate swappers), for instance, hold to a sexual fun philosophy in which sex is viewed as recreational or even athletic. Some people feel that sex is too restricted, even among those who are in love and share some form of personal and relational commitment. This hedonistic philosophy includes the view that virginity, chastity, and monogamy are outdated and to a degree nonsensical. Those who hold this philosophy—a true "playboy" philosophy of sexual anarchy—may believe it a "waste" to restrict oneself to one partner or to be virginal.

CONCLUSION

Sexual behavior has changed drastically through the ages, both in purpose and in character, from a strictly utilitarian purpose with procreation as a goal to having far different goals and objectives. But even with these different approaches to having sex, and from a position that many would consider to be behavior within the "normal" range, there are many who operate outside what are now considered acceptable parameters of sex, and violate the law in the process—individuals whose sexual behavioral patterns society has judged to be not only out of the normal but criminal as well.

3

Nuisance Sex Behaviors

There are many sexual behaviors that are completely aberrant to the senses of most Americans. These practices become more visible as scores of sex offenders are placed in correctional institutions throughout the United States. Sex offenders in prisons currently number over 62,000 (*Corrections Compendium*, January-February 1989, p. 9). Of course, the preponderance of those offenders are those who have been involved in rape and other violent sex crimes.

However, there is a growing measure of serious literature that suggests that many rapists, lust murderers, and sexually motivated serial murderers have histories of sexual behavior that reflect patterns that in the past have been considered only nuisances—not behaviors to become seriously concerned about (Holmes, 1983; Masters & Roberson, 1990, p. 378; K. McCarthy, 1984). Rosenfield (1985), for example, found that 62% of sex offenders in a prison sample revealed deviant sexual acts other than those for which they were sent to prison. They admitted to incest, frottage, voyeurism, and homosexuality. The latter three sexual acts and others that cause no obvious physical harm to the practitioner or the victim are called *nuisance sex behaviors*. This chapter is devoted to discussion of these sexual patterns.

17

Nuisance sex behaviors are often viewed in a less solemn fashion than sex crimes that cause serious trauma and death. But there may be great benefit in analyzing those who commit such nuisance sex acts; such analysis may indeed hold the key to the understanding of those who move into more serious types of sex offenses. While it may be true that Ted Bundy was a serial killer and a serial rapist who practiced anthropophagy and vampirism in addition to being a necrosadistic sex offender, Bundy admitted to me that he started off his sex crimes as a voyeur when he was 9 years old. Another sadistic killer admitted to me during an interview in prison that he also started peeping into the windows of women in his neighborhood when he was 9 years old. Neither of these two sexual serialists started their sexual crimes with rape and lust murder. They "progressed into degeneracy."

SCOPTOPHILIA

Scoptophiliacs (who are generally male), also known as voyeurs, receive sexual arousal by looking at private or intimate scenes. Money (1984) states that voyeurism is an allurement paraphilia. A *paraphilia* is an erotosexual condition of being recurrently responsive to, and obsessively dependent on, an unusual or unacceptable stimulus, perceptual or fantasy, in order to have a state of erotic arousal initiated or maintained and in order to achieve or facilitate orgasm, since it involves a segment of the preparatory phase of an erotic and sexual encounter (Money & Werlas, 1982). The *Diagnostic and Statistical Manual of Mental Disorders* (third edition, revised; DSM-III-R) attaches to this definition a time frame of "over a period of at least 6 months" (American Psychiatric Association, 1987).

Obviously, there are varying degrees in the nature of scoptophilia. Viewing X-rated videos or movies or reading hard-core pornography can be viewed as one form of voyeurism. Spying on people who are involved in sexual intercourse is quite another. But scoptophilia suggests that while voyeurism is indeed on a continuum, there are certain elements that set it apart from the "normal" act of viewing a beautiful body or a nude painting. Nearly all men will secretly peek into a window or through a keyhole in hopes of catching sight of a woman undressing, bathing, or interacting with a sexual partner. It would be a rare male who would not look at an attractive woman in a skimpy bathing suit at the beach (Haas & Haas, 1990, p. 552; Lahey, 1989, p. 527). Some voyeurs will go to great pains to capture a look—one man reportedly attached mirrors to his shoes to catch reflected images from under women's skirts.

Money (1984, 1985) states that the voyeur learns from experience and will look for scenes that he can easily visually invade. His erotic excitement is in the forbidden act of looking at off-limits scenes that are private. It is rare that the scoptophiliac will attempt to meet the victim or communicate with her. Typically, after the act occurs, the scoptophiliac will move to a place where he can masturbate.

Voyeurs typically are not exhibitionists, but Abel et al. (1988) report that in less than 2% of the cases they studied did voyeurs admit that they had only one paraphilia. The average number of paraphilias, including exhibitionism and frottage, was 4.8 per person. These authors also point out that in their study of 561 sex offenders, when multiple paraphilias existed in a single offender, one paraphilia initially was dominant. A second paraphilia then developed and overtook the first in dominance while the first continued for a number of months or even years, but at a greatly reduced intensity.

In each scoptophiliac's mental state, there will be a fantasy that may provide a script for behavior. In addition, as with many other sexual para-philias, voyeurism contains an overwhelming desire (*compulsion*) to spy upon a complete or virtual stranger who is in some stage of undress, having sexual intercourse, or in some other intimate situation (Freund & Blanchard, 1986). Many will take extreme steps to satisfy this "need" to invade the privacy of others.

But what kind of person is a voyeur? As stated above, it may be true that there is a little bit of voyeur in each of us. But for those whose fantasy and compulsive psychological factors override their better judgment, there appear to be some common characteristics.

Characteristics of the Voyeur

Voyeurs appear to be both sexually immature and frustrated (Chesser, 1971). Dwyer (1988) reports that often voyeurs deny they are sex offenders, have poor relationships with their fathers, have had overprotective mothers, have experienced early sexual trauma (which makes it more comfortable for them to see sex from afar), invoke religious justifications, lack sexual/social skills, have low self-esteem and high self-criticism, and do not take personal responsibility for their behavior. Other characteristics of voyeurs include great feelings of inadequacy and inferiority; also, many are quite young, often in their early 20s (Crooks & Baur, 1983, p. 595). Many are the youngest in their families. (See Table 3.1.)

Most voyeurs do not have serious criminal records, and, as a rule, they do not molest their victims (Katchadourian & Lunde, 1975). However, as

TABLE 3.1.   Traits of Scoptophiliacs

Sexually immature

Sexually frustrated

Poor relationship with father

Overprotective mother

Childhood sexual trauma

Poor social/sexual skills

Low self-esteem and high self-criticism

Young and chronic masturbator

---

mentioned above, some serious sex offenders have reportedly begun their careers as sex criminals as voyeurs. Ressler (1986) found that 71% of the sex-related murderers he studied reported early interests in voyeurism. It must be kept in mind that even though we view voyeurism as a nuisance sex act, there is ample serious research indicating that many times in later life men involved in this type of behavior move on to other types of paraphilias that become more serious and even more dangerous.

Triolism

One distinct form of scoptophilia is triolism. This paraphilia is a sexual pattern in which erotic stimulation is gained by watching oneself and/or others in sexual scenes. It appears from the literature that triolism may take several forms.

First of all, some triolists will gain sexual arousal and gratification from seeing themselves in some form of sexual scene. Some may photograph themselves in sexual acts. Jerry Brudos, a serial killer from Oregon, took pictures of himself in women's clothing, of his wife in the nude, and of his murdered victims. Ceiling mirrors, instant developing cameras, and video cameras may all be used by this type of paraphiliac in seeking sexual gratification (A. Ellis, 1986, pp. 26-28).

There are other triolists who seek pleasure by sharing a sexual partner with another person while the triolist looks on. An estimated 8 million couples have experienced this type of sexual behavior (Avery & Johannis, 1985, pp. 27-30). Triolism may also take the form of two couples having sexual relations at the same time in sight of each other. Swingers, or mate swappers, are often termed triolists. Sometimes women are forced into the swinging scene to fulfill the desires of their husbands, who may be triolists (Bowman, 1985, pp. 84-86; McCary, 1978, p. 334). Jenks (1985) reports that swingers are generally nondescript members of the community, but there are some characteristics those in his study tended to have in common: They were relatively new to the community, had moved often in the past five years, were members of the middle class, were conservative in their political views, identified little with religion, and belonged to more community groups than nonswingers.

There are basically two types of swingers, open and closed. Open swingers join national and local swinging clubs and have a wide range of sexual partners. Joining a club such as Select or Kindred Spirits, the swinging couple is exposed to a large number of persons who are potential partners (Crewdson, 1988, pp. 98-99). Closed swingers, on the other hand, have sexual experiences with only a few people, usually personal acquaintances.

Swinging cuts across socioeconomic lines—construction workers, physicians, nurses, professors, ministers, housewives, engineers, and others are represented in the triolist population. It is their preoccupation with sex that distinguishes them from the nonswinging population (Avery & Johannis, 1985, p. 30). The fun moralist, the swinger, sees sex for the sake of pleasure, and can decompartmentalize sex from love.

There may also be a homosexual element in mate swapping. Sadock, Kaplan, and Freedman (1976) report that the husband can see another male sexually active with his partner and in this way a small percentage of men can take the opportunity to explore various homosexual impulses (see also Money & Musaph, 1977). Holmes (1972), D. Dixon (1985), and J. Dixon (1985) report that in most cases the husband forces the wife into swinging, but then it is the wife in most cases who wants to continue.

Triolism seldom comes to the attention of those in law enforcement or counseling unless it affects family or personal functioning. Since so many are "in the closet," it is not known what the full impact of triolism is on sexual functioning. Obviously, a case such as Brudos's is not at all typical of the many others who are involved in this type of paraphilia. Swinging, as a form of triolism, has been studied, but it does not appear to be a form of behavior that is, by itself, necessarily detrimental to the family (D. Dixon, 1985; J. Dixon, 1985; Holmes, 1972). However, it may be that swinging is on the decline and may soon become obsolete (Fang, 1976). The risk of AIDS and other venereal diseases certainly has an influence on the behavior of some triolists as to their decision to become involved in an intimate fashion with total strangers (Haas & Haas, 1990, pp. 321-322).

EXHIBITIONISM

Exhibitionism is the deliberate exposure of one's genitals under inappropriate circumstances. Typically, the exhibitionist (usually male) will expose himself to female strangers in public places, such as in parks, at bus stops, and in school yards. Exhibitionists are typically young, and many start their episodes when they are in their teens. While no one knows the exact number of such offenders in American society, it is estimated that as many as 40 million women a year are victims of exhibitionism (Cox & Maletsky, 1980).

The exact reasons exhibitionists expose themselves are unclear. One theory is that the act of exposure, accompanied by masturbation, serves as a means of reducing stress. Of course, sexual excitement from the exposure itself should not be ruled out. Another theory is that the exhibitionist has been somehow damaged by a female and he is lashing out against all women in the hope that his psyche can be restored. Yet another theory is that the exhibitionist suffers from extreme feelings of personal inadequacy and a low sense of masculinity, and needs affirmation to reinforce these feelings. Some theorize that the exhibitionist feels anger and resentment toward people in general and women in particular. The exhibitionist's intent, in directing the attention of others toward his genitals, is to shock and degrade these persons.

For the exhibitionist, the sexual act is not intercourse, but exposure. By shocking the female victim, the exhibitionist reinforces the sense of power he needs for personal fulfillment. Having exposed himself to someone, the exhibitionist will often go to a private place in order to masturbate.

The reaction of the female victim is important to the exhibitionist. If she is frightened, the exhibitionist experiences sexual excitement and is impelled to masturbate. It is very rare for such a paraphiliac to have any type of direct physical relationship with a female to whom he has exposed himself. If a female victim responds to an exhibitionist in a sexual manner, he will typically be bewildered, because the victim is not behaving in the way that he thinks she should; he is likely to run away (Knox, 1984, p. 397). Abel (1981), however, reports that there may be some exhibitionists who do move into direct confrontation with women. Although no absolute relationship between exhibitionism and further sex crimes has been found, it is clear that some offenders do move from this type of crime to more serious ones.

TRANSVESTISM

The transvestite is typically a heterosexual male, often married, who dresses in the clothes of the other sex initially because of sexual reasons. Many transvestites start their cross-dressing at an early age, and the cross-dressing itself is accompanied by masturbation.

Many transvestites, often incorrectly termed fetishists, have learned to deal with their sexual proclivity and seldom come into contact with the criminal justice system. A social worker in an emergency room at the University of Louisville Humana Hospital told me that more than a few times she has attended male auto accident victims who, when their outer clothes were removed, were revealed to be wearing panties, bras, garter belts, and other items of women's apparel.

As stated above, the transvestite typically commences cross-dressing at an early age, and the cross-dressing becomes intimately attached to sexual feelings. The Tri-S (Society for the Second Self), a national self-help group for transvestites, states that after a few years, the transvestite recognizes that there is another dimension to cross-dressing. For a short period of time, while dressed in women's clothing, the cross-dresser retreats to the world of the female, a world in which he perceives there is little stress. In that time, he is in a world where there are few demands made on him, unlike the demands he faces in his male world.

Jerry Brudos is a transvestite. He had a fetish for women's high-heeled shoes and wore a pair that he stole from one of his victims (Stack, 1983). He also insisted that his wife wear these shoes and even made at least one of his murdered victims wear the shoes immediately before he killed her. After killing four women, Brudos was arrested and sent to the Oregon State Penitentiary. (I have seen him in the visiting room at the prison on two occasions but he refuses to speak to me.)

It would be a mistake, however, to assume that all transvestites are sex offenders and that many come into contact with the criminal justice system as did Jerry Brudos. It is unlikely that this is the case. It is also unlikely that anyone can accurately estimate the number of men who are transvestites. This is a hidden sexual behavior.

SCATOPHILIA

There appears to be some disagreement regarding the similarities between exhibitionists and those involved in making obscene telephone calls (scatophiliacs). In scatophilia, however, the acts are more aggressive and yet more distant than in exhibitionism (Nadler, 1968). The erotic gratification is gained from the narrations that transpire between the caller and the victim rather than from any form of genital sex.

In both cases, offenders typically are male, inadequate, with problems in developing relationships, feelings of isolation, perceptions of their fathers being "supermen," and feelings that their mothers never loved them (Oliver, 1974; Wark, 1982). Also in both cases, the act of either deliberately exposing himself or making an obscene telephone call is the only manner in which the paraphiliac can express himself sexually. Matek (1988) reports that imagery plays an important role for obscene phone callers. Some scatophiliacs may cross-dress to increase the sexual excitement (Dalby, 1988). Fantasy plays a large role; the caller hears the victim but does not see her. The telephone connection itself provides a pseudointimate scenario (Greenberg, Bruess, Mullen, & Sands, 1989b, p. 535; Matek, 1988).

Like the exhibitionist, the scatophiliac wants his victim, the person on the other end of the phone line, to be shocked, disgusted, or horrified by his demeanor or words. The scatophiliac is dependent on this reaction for erotic arousal, and to facilitate or achieve orgasm through masturbation (Crooks & Baur, 1983; Money, 1980).

Of course, not all obscene phone callers are alike. Murray and Beran (1968) report five types of callers: obscene, anonymous, humorous, witty, and miscellaneous. (As a university professor, I receive several phone calls at the end of each semester when I assign grades, some of which I place in the obscene category because of the negative remarks the callers make about my parental background.) Leising (1985) categorizes three other types of callers: the chronic caller who is open about his reasons for calling (sexual), the caller who begins with a believable sexual problem but then becomes graphic or vulgar, and the sexually abusive caller who describes in a cold, detached manner how he raped or assaulted a female victim.

The obscene telephone caller typically makes his calls by dialing random phone numbers. Fortunately, obscene callers seldom make personal contact with persons they have called. However, Ressler (1986a) reports that in his sample of murderers who rape and mutilate, 22% reported interest in obscene phone calls; he does not mention what percentage of his sample followed up in making such calls. It appears, in any case, that the danger of the obscene phone caller is minimal. Of course, this may be of little comfort to his victims (Dannemeyer, 1988; Mano, 1985).

If a person is victimized by an obscene caller, the telephone company can provide a pen register, which records the number called from to a party's phone or a polarity trap, which locks in the two numbers until the telephone company chooses to release the phones. In Indiana, a device that displays the telephone number of an incoming call has come under attack by some citizens and private groups. It is their position that use of this device, Caller ID, would constitute an unconstitutional invasion of privacy and would pose special problems for shelters for battered women and social service hot lines. However, the proponents of this device state that it would help the police in apprehending obscene telephone callers. In 1990, a Pennsylvania court ruled that Caller ID constituted an invasion of privacy and a violation of the state's wiretapping laws. It appears that the courts will have to rule on the constitutionality of the device. Without such a mechanism, however, the one-time obscene phone call is virtually impossible to trace.

Technology has made it easier for the obscene phone caller. Professional narrators are employed by such companies as the Erotic Telephone Network and Bad Girls. These dial-a-porn services make up a multimillion-dollar industry (Weir, 1987). In New York, for example, one such service paid the phone company $25,000 a day for subscriber service. The New York Telephone Co. earns about $15 million a year from such payments. The service companies themselves also spend millions of dollars in advertising (Mano, 1985). Dannemeyer (1988) found that the average cost to the consumer of live sex phone calls is $6, and the average cost for a recorded obscene message is $3.85. (Parents are often concerned about their children making calls to commercial dial-a-porn services; they may now have their phone companies block any calls from their phones to 900 or 976 numbers.)

FROTTAGE

A frotteur is a paraphiliac who realizes sexual gratification from rubbing against certain body parts of another person. Often, this occurs when the victim, typically a stranger, is in a crowded but public place, such as a shopping center, elevator, or subway (Campbell, 1989, p. 294). Frotteurs experience fantasies that are accompanied by strong, irresistible urges to touch others. The fantasies often center on the victims' wishes to have a caring, affectionate relationship with the frotteur (American Psychiatric Association, 1987, p. 283).

The process of toucherism (another name for frottage) includes the fantasy, the urge to touch, the selection of a victim, the touching itself, and then fleeing to a place where masturbation usually occurs. Included in the process of offending is an escape plan. The victim selected fits the frotteur's ideal victim type (IVT). The victim is viewed as sexually attractive, usually wearing tight-fitting clothes. The frotteur rubs his genitals against the victim's thighs or buttocks or fondles her genitalia or breasts (American Psychiatric Association, 1987, p. 283). Victims often are amazed that this could be happening in public. In more than a few cases, victims may indeed reciprocate (Money, 1984).

The frotteur typically starts his behavior by adolescence, and most of the acts occur when the offender is between the ages of 15 and 25. This type of sexual disorder is found in such a pronounced degree only in males; frotteurs are often intelligent, and most belong to the middle and upper classes. As is the case with many other types of paraphiliacs, frotteurs often have other types of paraphilias as well. Abel et al. (1988) report that the "average" frotteur has almost four other sexual "perversions."

It does not appear that the frotteur is a great danger to society. However, the treatment of such offenders does not offer a great deal of optimism for change. It may be a reasonable concern that frotteurs may move into other types of sexual behaviors that offer more danger to others.

KLISMAPHILIA

Klismaphilia is sexual arousal linked with being given an enema, either in fantasy or in actuality (Bartol, 1986; Cooper & Sacks, 1986). The klismaphiliac has become erotically aroused by the eliminatory function. How an individual becomes involved in klismaphilia is unknown. Lesee (1984) reports that it is often possible to pin down an early history of too much ado about enema in the infancy of those who as adults practice this form of erotic behavior (see also Money, 1984).

Males especially are excited by klismaphilia and experience erections when they are administered enemas as youths (Haas & Haas, 1990; Knox, 1984, p. 403). But there are also women who are involved in this form of sexual behavior and who use it as a masturbatory device. This paraphilia is a substitute for genital intercourse.

The klismaphiliac can lead a normal life, with no one suspecting this particularly sexual interest (Denko, 1973). Klismaphiliacs often indulge in their taste privately and secretly; at most, they may try to get others (usually females) to administer an occasional enema under the guise of constipation and attempt to conceal their pleasure from the administrator (Stoller, 1986, p. 6). But there are other devotees who involve themselves in klismaphilia in a variety of homosexual, transvestite, sadomasochistic, and other settings. Those in this group do not want to change, nor do they feel any form of shame because of their behavior (unlike those in the first group) (Denko, 1976).

There is no waning of interest in this form of sexual behavior. In fact, with the current focus on variant sexual practices, klismaphilia will probably become more widely discussed and perhaps more widely practiced (Denko, 1976).

BESTIALITY

A common sexual theme found in pornography is that of bestiality, or sex with animals. Early history shows that bestiality has been long chronicled. In ancient Greece a moral creature was one who obeyed his impulses. If sex was desired and no human being with a suitable orifice was available, a horse, mule, or deer was considered suitable (Dover, 1986). In 1300 A.D., an English law made sex with animals a capital offense. This was later changed to life imprisonment, and then amended to 10 years in prison (Crew, 1986, pp. 70-71; Parker, 1987, p. 663). In early colonial America, Thomas Grange was burned to death for alleged crimes against a mare, a cow, two goats, five sheep, two calves, and a turkey. Recent reports from Los Angeles tell of a man who, after fights with his girlfriend, sought revenge by raping her pet chicken. After the second incident, the chicken died (Bullough, 1988).

Bestiality occurs in either sex. With a male, for example, there may be an insistence on an animal performing oral sex upon him or manual manipulation by the male upon the animal. With the female, an animal may perform sexual intercourse, cunnilingus, or other forms of physical behavior. Another form of bestiality is termed *formicophilia*. In this paraphilia, sexual arousal comes from small creatures—ants, snails, and the like—crawling on a person's nipples or genitals (Dewaraja, 1987; Dewaraja & Money, 1986). Zoophilia is different from bestiality in that it includes no actual sexual contact with the animal. Contact with the animal itself takes the form of stroking or fondling only (Campbell, 1989, p. 810).

How prevalent is bestiality? It has been reported that 17% of rural males have at some time experienced orgasm with an animal (Ammons & Ammons, 1987). The most common animals involved have been calves, sheep, dogs, cats, geese, and hens. Bestiality is perhaps best viewed as an act committed by many people, but typically when there is no suitable human partner. Although it does not involve a significant number of people, it continues to be an outlet for some.

PYGMALIONISM

The name of this sexual paraphilia comes from the classic story of Pygmalion, who fell in love with a statue he had himself made. Pygmalionism is a sexual attraction to a statue (agalmatophilia), doll, or mannequin. The inflatable doll, the collapsible doll, and other such items are very popular in adult bookstores. Pygmalionists may be persons who are, for one reason or another, unable to relate personally and sexually to other human beings. They have power and control over the inanimate object, and, moreover, the object can never reject their advances.

Technology has made many advances that can aid persons who have atypical sexual interests. In the case of the pygmalionist, for example, some of the more expensive dolls available have cassette players located within their "bodies" that can be used to play tapes that utter obscene words or phrases (coprophilia).

GERONTOPHILIA

Gerontophilia is the use of an elderly person as a sexual object. This paraphilia is not easy to detect because of cultural influences that affect mate selection. For example, it is not uncommon for a woman to marry a much older man. It may indeed be that there is sometimes a financial element to this choice of partner.

When a young man assaults elderly women, this falls into the category of sadistic gerontosexuality (Ellis & Abarbanel, 1967). Typically, this type of offender manifests the following traits: obsessive personality, a history of enuresis until about the age of 25, a lack of interest in younger women, an inability to contain impulses, and a tendency to be violent and aggressive sexually (Oules, Boscredon, & Bataille, 1977). Additional characteristics include a need for power or a sadistic intent to do physical damage.

Rapes of elderly women are rare; only about 3% of all rapes involve victims over the age of 50. But when an elderly woman is raped there is a stronger threat to life, and this attack often results in the murder of the victim (Bopp, 1987). The psychopathology of those who molest and murder older victims is more pronounced than that of those who assault younger women (Pollack, 1988). The incidence of this paraphilia is quite rare, but when it does occur in men, it often becomes dangerous. In women, the motivations behind gerontophilia are usually quite different; the gains are more often material than psychological.

MYSOPHILIA

Mysophilia is an erotic interest in filth. While some professionals believe this is a form of masochism—it is difficult to imagine that someone can be aroused by what many persons consider to be repugnant—it is indeed true that dirt, feces, and so on are erotically arousing to some. Some men, for example, are aroused by women's soiled underwear (McCary, 1978). Even erotic vomiting has been reported (Stoller, 1982). Hazelwood, Dietz, and Burgess (1983) tell of a young man who inserted a corn cob into his rectum and then walked outside, dug a hole, and made mud using a garden hose. He then covered himself with mud and engaged in autoerotic asphyxia (for a discussion of autoeroticism, see Chapter 6).

Mysophilia is also found in the forms of coprolagnia and urolagnia, in which erotic gratification is associated with feces and urine, respectively. The practice of urolagnia can take place by one person urinating into the mouth or onto the body of another person. Prevalent in the homosexual community, the practitioners are called "golden shower" devotees. In some major cities there are urolagniac clubs, where members hold meetings to engage in various "water sports," including urinating on each other and drinking urine (Shelp, 1987). Haas and Haas (1990, p. 557) report that about 4% of men and women have experienced "golden showers." One reported case involved a 17-year-old boy who ate snow contaminated by horse and cow urine, and, while working as a part-time janitor in a school, drank from unflushed toilets (Dense, 1982, pp. 336-338).

Coprolagnia has been reported for years. Chesser (1971) tells of a Russian nobleman who insisted that his mistress defecate upon his chest. Another man had prostitutes relieve themselves in a golden saucer, and he would eat the feces with a golden spoon. Recently a nurse died after being admitted to a hospital two previous times for a serious illness. After a thorough police investigation, it was ascertained that she had been injecting into her arm a mixture of water and the feces of her pet parrot.

Coprolagnia is not only a perverse form of sexual behavior, at least in the view of most people, but it can also be quite dangerous to the health of the practitioner because of the bacteria in feces and other potential health problems. Urolagnia, however, poses no great health hazard. Urine from an otherwise healthy person is sterile and poses no great health concern. In the military, for example, the drinking of one's own urine is taught as a survival technique.

CONCLUSION

There are many kinds of sexual expression that members of a society approve or condemn. This chapter has dealt with behaviors that are probably considered by most to be either matters of personal preference or at least not vital societal concerns. In the next chapter, however, far more far-reaching forms of sexual expression will be discussed: incest and pedophilia. These two sexual behaviors directed against children must be viewed in a most serious fashion. The focus of Chapter 4 is, in every case, on the child as victim.

4

Sex Crimes Against Children

There are few things viewed as more obscene and that provoke as much public outrage as sex crimes against children. Incest and pedophilia are two such crimes. The incidence of both appears to have increased dramatically in the past several years, or perhaps an increase in the reporting of such crimes accounts for their apparent rapid and pandemic increase. Kinsey, for example, found in 1953 that approximately 24% of his female subjects had established sexual contacts before adolescence (Ellis & Abarbanel, 1973, p. 265). In a probably more scientific study conducted recently, it was estimated that almost 20% of all children, regardless of gender, will experience some form of sexual abuse before their eighteenth birthdays (O'Brien & Goldstein, 1988). The figures vary widely from study to study: Wyatt (1985) found that almost 50% of young women between the ages of 18 and 36 had been sexually abused prior to the age of 18; another study showed a much lower abuse rate, 10% (Baker & Duncan, 1985). However, regardless of the numbers of children who are sexually victimized, the problem must be considered a monumentally important one.

There is no more vulnerable victim available to an adult than a powerless child. This is especially true when the child is abused by a caretaker—a parent or stepparent, a grandparent, an uncle or aunt. It may well be the case that the child molester victimizes children because it allows him or her to feel powerful (Araji & Finkelhor, 1985, p. 21).

This chapter will explore two types of sex crimes against children, one perpetrated within the family and one that takes place outside the family. While sexual child abuse is the focus here, it is worth noting that other forms of physical child abuse appear to be more prevalent among younger children, while sexual abuse is more prevalent among older children, especially as they approach the early teen years. Age, then, seems to designate the type of abuse that might befall a child.

There is great concern among law enforcement officials and others regarding the numbers of missing children who may indeed be victims of violent child molesters. To date, however, there has been no nationwide, comprehensive study conducted to measure adequately not only the number of abused children but also the number of missing children. To determine this number, the Office of Juvenile Justice and Delinquency Prevention plans to sponsor a national survey of 40,000 households in all types of residential settings (see Exhibit 4.1). The results of this study should give us a better picture of the true circumstances of the children who are often thought to be victims of all pedophiles, including aggressive and sadistic child offenders. The goals of this effort include determining for the first time the following information:

(1) the number of children missing
(2) the types of children most likely to be missing
(3) the circumstances surrounding the disappearances
(4) what happens to them while they are gone

This is a truly monumental effort, and one that, if successful, will shed new light on the very serious social problem of child sexual abuse.

PEDOPHILIA

Sexual contact with children outside the family is viewed as one of the most abominable actions an adult can perpetrate upon a child. This abuser, a pedophile, is often called a "lover of children," although this is not a popular definition. Pedophiles are more often called child molesters. I will use the term *pedophile* here because there is often more to the behavioral pattern of

Exhibit 4.1

The OJJDP Study on Missing Children Will Include . . .

analysis of FBI data on the number of children who have been abducted and murdered by strangers

analysis of data on children who have been abandoned or forced from their homes

study of law enforcement agency records of kidnappings abductions and related crimes against children

interviews with returned runaways

survey of residential facilities to determine how many residents run away

---

this kind of offender than simply the molestation of a child. Thomas (1985, p. 1246) states that pedophilia is a fondness for children, an unnatural desire for sexual relations with children. If one accepts this definition, it is easy to see the overwhelming difficulty it implies for the treatment and possible rehabilitation of such offenders.

Sexual interest in children is perhaps not as infrequent as we would like to believe. In Briere's (1989) sample of 193 male undergraduate students, 21% reported sexual attraction involving children, 9% described sexual fantasies involving children, 5% admitted to having masturbated to such fantasies, and 7% indicated some likelihood of having sex with a child if they could avoid detection and punishment.

The basic etiology of pedophilia is unknown. Salter (1989) suggests that there are a number of predisposing factors that cause a person to become a child molester. Offenders sometimes have deviant arousal patterns that make them sexually attracted to children, but for others child molestation may be their way of acting out responses to nonsexual problems. Tingle, Bernard, Robbins, and Newman (1986) found that pedophiles most often come from homes with domineering mothers and passive or even missing fathers. Glasser (1988) suggests that as a result of their sexual deviation, pedophiles are unable to identify with others, may create a false self, and struggle with intense but unrecognized guilt.

Pedophiles are typically male, but this is not always the case. Indeed, Condy, Templer, Brown, and Veaco (1987) suggest that women who molest children are a great deal more prevalent than is typically thought. Often, when a woman is accused of sexually molesting an underaged child, there are social values that impede her arrest and prosecution. Recently, for example, a female high school teacher was arrested and charged with having an illicit sexual exchange with three of her young male students, all under the age of 15. The jury found the woman innocent of all charges. Incredibly, one father remarked that his son should consider himself lucky to have had a sexual experience with an older woman.

Situational Characteristics of Pedophiles

Contrary to the public perception, the pedophile rarely physically harms the child unless the molester is a mysoped. It is a myth that all pedophiles cause either physical or emotional permanent damage. This is a controversial statement that many will disagree with—Robert Hain, of the Louisville, Kentucky, Police Department, for example, has stated his belief that approximately 30% of all molested children will themselves become molesters (personal communication, October 4, 1990). However, it appears that the reactions of the child's significant others (particularly the parents) have more of a negative psychological impact than the experience with the pedophile. Also, there appear to be few pedophiles who use either physical or verbal force (aggressive child offenders) (Haas & Haas, 1990).

The majority of heterosexual pedophiles are neither senile nor mentally defective. They tend to be conservative and moralistic, and some even require alcohol before they can commit their offenses. Dr. Al C. Carlisle (personal communication, May 1990), psychologist at the Utah State Prison, estimates that a single offender may molest as many as 300 children in his lifetime. Pedophiles usually do not have criminal records, with the exception of possible previous convictions for molesting children. In Kentucky, for example, a well-respected physician, Dr. Fred Rainey, once the president of the Kentucky Medical Association and the state Jaycees, elected vice president of the U.S. Jaycees (and in 1965 came within 5 votes of being elected the national president), and awarded the honor of Citizen-Doctor of the Year, pleaded guilty to abusing seven teenagers between 1959 and 1988. The victims—four females and three males—said they were 13 to 17 years old at the times of the offenses. Rainey has entered the Alford plea, and is currently awaiting sentencing.

Seduction is typically the ploy used in gaining sexual entry with children. In Lahey's (1989) study, young girls were modally the victims of pedophiles. However, other studies show that nonincarcerated sex offenders sexually molest young boys with an incidence that is five times greater than their molestation of young girls. Again, it is typical for the child and the pedophile to know each other before the molestation occurs, and the more familiar they become, the more oral-genital and genital-to-genital activity will occur (Holmes, 1983).

Regardless of the type of pedophile, many do indeed have adult sexual outlets. Many are married. Some have been known to marry women with children in order to have access to the children; this molestation is typically classified as incest, because of the victim's relationship to the pedophile. But there may indeed be "serial pedophiles" who marry more than once to gain access to children.

Types of Pedophiles

Pedophiles are not all alike. They differ, for example, in their preferences for sexual victims regarding age and sex. Based upon this differentiation, a typology of pedophiles can be formulated based upon victim selectivity, type of sexual activity, and motivation (see Table 4.1).

An initial typology of pedophilia is based upon the preferred age of the victim. Most pedophiles have an age-span preference of three to four years. That is to say that pedophiles, like the overwhelming number of sex offenders, are age specific (as in the case of Dr. Rainey, mentioned above). If the preferred victim is, for instance, 9 years of age, the child offender will typically select a child somewhere in the age range of 7 to 11.

Pedophiles are usually interested in children who have not yet reached puberty. Child sexual offenders who are interested in victims who have reached puberty are termed *hebephiles*. The hebephile is a person who would not think of having a sexual encounter with a child who has not reached puberty.

The sex of the child also plays an integral part in the selection of the victim. Typically, pedophiles select victims based on sex as well as age. A sexual child offender will usually choose as victims either always males or always females; it is very unusual for a pedophile to molest both boys and girls, although it is not unheard of. The case of Wayne Williams raises some questions regarding victim selection. Williams, often called the Atlanta Child Killer, was convicted of the murders of two adults, a 21-year-old and a

TABLE 4.1. Typology of Child Molesters

Element	Immature Offender	Regressed Offender	Sadistic Offender	Fixated Offender
Harmful to the Child	No	No	Yes	No
Aggressive Personality	No	No	Yes	No
Antisocial Personality	No	No	Yes	No
Child Sexual Preference	No	Yes	Yes	Yes
Knows the Child	Yes	No	No	Yes
Intercourse Occurs	No	Yes	Yes	Yes

27-year-old. He was suspected of the murders of children from the age of 7 to the age of Nathaniel Cater, the 27-year-old. Also, there were both males and females on the list of victims, an usual circumstance. Incidentally, Williams has never been charged with any of the killings of young children in Atlanta.

It is important to note that the sexual preference of the pedophile does not necessarily reflect his adult sexual orientation. Many times, the police will arrest a pedophile who molests young males and then discover that the child offender is married and has children of his own. Law enforcement professionals often become confused because they tend to believe that if a child molester abuses males he must be homosexual. This is simply not necessarily the case.

The Mysoped

There are some pedophiles who are intent on molesting children with the express desire to harm their victims physically. This type of pedophile, who is usually male, has made a vital connection between sexual arousal and fatal violence. Typically, the child is a stranger to this aggressive and sadistic child offender. It appears also that this offender may stalk the child, rather than use any form of seduction (the method typical of many pedophiles).

The mysoped will often abduct a child from places where children gather: playgrounds, schools, shopping centers, and other such places. He will usually not attempt to seduce or otherwise induce the child to go with him; he simply takes the child by force. The abduction is followed by a scenario that includes pain inflicted upon the child, followed by the child's death.

This type of pedophile has no "love" of children in the traditional sense. He is interested only in causing harm and death to a vulnerable victim to whom he feels greatly superior. The mysoped inflicts fatal physical harm on the victim and often mutilates the victim's body. If the victim is a young boy, the child's penis may be cut off and inserted into the child's mouth. Small girls are also brutally assaulted, and the physical assault is often directed toward the child's genitals. This sexual sadist often terrorizes the child with some type of weapon, and the crime is premeditated and ritualized. There is a great deal of sadomasochism involved with this type of offender, with the usual end being the death of the child (Burgess, Holstrom, Sgroi, & Groth, 1978).

The Regressed Child Offender

The regressed offender is one who has historically been involved with adults in "normal" sexual relationships. Psychologically, this type of child offender experiences the child as a pseudoadult (Burgess et al., 1978). Typically married or in a long-standing relationship, this sex offender is often launched into a sexual act or series of sexual acts with children because of some situational precipitating cause. Witness the case of Tony A:

> I had never thought of molesting children. I was a deacon in my church, a Cub Scout leader, and a youth minister. I had been around children all my life with no intent to harm them. One day I came home from work and my wife said that there was something she wanted to talk to me about. She said, " Tony, you physically disgust me and I never want you to touch me again!" This really affected me as you can imagine. In the next two weeks, I was coming up for a big promotion and I knew that if I did not get it I would never be promoted before I retired. I'm 60 years old and this would have been my last shot. It came down to me and a young fellow at work who was only 30 years old. He got the job.

> I was crushed. That weekend I and the Cub Scout troop went on a scouting trip. As usual there were two people to a pup tent, and there was a young 9-year-old sharing a tent with me. It started raining and thundering and the boy got scared. He asked if he could come over to my side of the tent and climb into my sleeping

bag. Well, one thing led to another and before long I was fondling him. This led to other young boys, which went on for over a year. (author's files)

Tony was finally discovered and arrested. This offender, like others in the regressed category, had a normal history, including an adolescence with good peer relationships and experiences. Because of some situation or occurrence in his life—a poor job performance review, an unfaithful wife, some social maladjustment, or whatever—the regressed offender develops feelings of inadequacy that frequently result in alcoholism as well as child molestation.

This offender typically prefers children he does not know. Usually the child is female. Of course, this was not the case with Tony, but small boys were available to him. His victims were victims of opportunity.

In prison, Tony joined a sex offenders' treatment program and was successful in obtaining parole. He is now back in his own community, but he has lost his job and his wife, and he is working at a menial job despite having a graduate degree in mechanical engineering.

Compared with other child sexual offenders, the regressed child offender has the best chance of not reoffending, especially if the precipitating situational causes can be discovered and remedied.

The Fixated Child Offender

This child offender has not really developed past the point where he, as a child, found children attractive and desirable. In other words, he has become "fixed" at an early stage of psychosexual development (Burgess et al., 1978). The fixated type of child molester's pedophiliac interest started in adolescence; unlike the case of regressed child offenders, there is no precipitating cause in his child abuse. His interest in children is persistent and compulsive. Male victims are the preferred target of abuse.

The fixated child offender has little or no activity with agemates, usually is single, and is considered to be immature and uncomfortable around other adults (Burgess et al., 1978). This offender becomes as a child in his life-style and behaviors. Burg (1983) found that many pedophiles select children as sexual objects because youths are less demanding, more easily dominated, and less critical of their partners' performance than are adults.

The fixated child offender is not interested in physically harming the child. He loves children and does not desire to do anything that might harm them. He courts a child, buys the child gifts as a seduction ploy, and slowly becomes physically intimate with the child. Oral-genital sex is the norm, and actual intercourse develops only after a generous period of time has passed.

The Naive Pedophile

Many child offenders are incorrectly diagnosed as having some type of brain dysfunction, such as senility. There are obviously some pedophiles who fall into this category, but most do not. Only a few child offenders are involved with children because they do not understand the true nature of their offenses or the societal rules prohibiting the involvement of adults with children in a sexual manner. There may indeed be some who suffer from some type of organic problem or senility and are unable to appreciate the impact of what they have done. The elderly grandfather or the older gentleman who lives down the street may suffer from impaired intellectual functioning and not understand the ramifications of his actions. This offender often merely likes to hug, fondle, kiss, lick, or stroke a child, with no intent to attempt sexual intercourse.

Pedophile Organizations

Child sex is a topic that immediately raises the ire of most Americans. Many are adamantly opposed to any mercy for those who intentionally and with full mental capacities sexually abuse children. However, there are more than a few groups that not only favor child sex but have joined forces with others who share their point of view. Perhaps the three most famous groups are the Rene Guyon Society, the North American Man/Boy Love Association (NAMBLA), and the Childhood Sensuality Circle (DeYoung, 1989).

The Rene Guyon Society is a national association of persons who are vitally interested in promoting legislation that would permit adults to have sex with children. Indeed, the group's motto reflects its attitude: "Sex Before Eight or Else It's Too Late!" Tim O'Hara, national spokesman for the society, repeatedly states that none of the members of the society has anything to do with breaking the law regarding sex with children. O'Hara states that children should be allowed to involve themselves with older men, especially members of the society. But because children suffer from too much "body guilt," they are prohibited from sex with adults. Conversely, adult males should be allowed to have sexual relations with children, but they too suffer from body guilt. The way out of this dilemma is to have sex as a child with an adult.

NAMBLA is another organization that promotes childhood sex. This organization maintains its organizational headquarters in New York City and has chapters in San Francisco, Los Angeles, Boston, and Toronto, as well as other cities. NAMBLA was founded, according to its publications, as a response to the "extreme oppression of men and boys involved in consensual sex and other relationships with each other." Obviously this organization caters primarily to homosexuals who prefer to have sex with young boys (DeYoung, 1989). The *NAMBLA Bulletin*, the organization's newsletter, contains news, letters from members, ads, and other items for its members.

The Childhood Sensuality Circle, of San Diego, California, is another American group that has as its goal to change the laws regarding sex with children. Lesser known than the other two groups, this organization is equally vigorous in its activities to change the sex laws.

Summary

In order to combat the very serious threat that pedophilia poses for the children of our nation, we must gain an understanding of the types, behavioral patterns, gains, and motives of this type of serious sex offender. Finkelhor and Araji (1986) suggest that four elements should be of concern when pedophiles' interests and behaviors are studied:

(1) *emotional congruence:* why the adult has an emotional need to relate to a child

(2) *sexual arousal:* why the adult can become sexually aroused by a child

(3) *blockage:* why alternative sources of sexual and emotional gratification are not available

(4) *disinhibition:* why the adult is not deterred by normal prohibitions

If we can discover more about these four factors in pedophilic behavior, we may be able to protect our children more effectively.

INCEST

Incest is typically defined as sexual intercourse between family members. Many believe that this definition should be widened to include other types of sexual acts as well, such as sodomy, fondling, oral sex, and other intimate behaviors.

Historically, incest has been viewed negatively. Disgust and aversion are common reactions to incest. At certain times in certain societies, however—in ancient Egypt and among certain Native American tribes, for instance—incest has been not only accepted but encouraged. Incest has not always been considered to be an act perpetrated by an adult upon a vulnerable child and thus universally condemned. Even in the twentieth century, certain theorists, including Freud, have believed that the child provokes the act because of sexual attraction to the parent and underlying sexual conflict.

The extent of incest in American society is unknown. Barry (1984) estimates that between 60,000 and 100,000 female children are sexually abused within their families each year, but only 20% of these cases are reported. Harrington (1986) reports that from 1940 to 1970, 1% of the women in her sample had experienced sexual contact with their fathers or stepfathers. Ringwalt, Christopher, and Earp (1988) found that approximately 1 woman in 40 has been sexually abused by her father. Even more astounding is their finding that in a survey of 500 psychiatrists, 52% indicated that daughters usually contribute to the incest. This is not a statement with which most professionals would agree. Other studies estimate that the extent of incest ranges from 7% of the U.S. population to more than 38%; many of these studies use college-age populations, and one weakness they share is in underrepresenting lower socioeconomic levels (Fritz, Stoll, & Wagner, 1981; Salter, 1989).

Who Are the Perpetrators?

According to Wyatt (1985), 16% of incest perpetrators are uncles, cousins, brothers, fathers, or grandfathers; most are cousins or uncles. Another 16% are stepfathers, foster fathers, or boyfriends of the victims' mothers. About 2% of cases of incest involve the victim's biological father. Barry (1984) states that the brother-sister incestuous relationship is the most common, but the situation that captures most of the headlines is the father-daughter relationship.

Perhaps the least-discussed incestuous relationship is that between mother and child (see Exhibit 4.2). While Barry (1984) suggests that this is very rare, O'Grady (1988) claims that it is a great deal more prevalent than once thought. It may be that reported cases of female incest offenders are quite rare because women are usually considered to be sexually harmless to children. However, some women do have incestuous relationships with their children, for various reasons. McCarty (1986) says that mothers who are incest offenders often come from abusive backgrounds (both sexual and physical), suffer from psychotic episodes, and have histories of substance

Exhibit 4.2

Sleep

Thunder raged across my bed,
Screams emitted from my head.
Daddy please come and tell me
   it's okay
Dreams of bunnies
   instead of snakes today.
Boxes, boxes capturing me.
Let me out was my plea.
Here comes mother instead.
I wish I lay here dead.

           —BJ

SOURCE: Reprinted by permission of Parents United, Louisville, Kentucky, chapter.

abuse; most are at least average in intelligence. She further adds that incest is used often as a substitute for a missing husband.

The Psychology of the Incest Offender

A great deal of research has been done examining the dynamics behind the reasons for incest. Nanjundappa (1987) found that in a sample of juvenile incest offenders, the perpetrators came from homes where there was a great deal of physical or sexual violence, substance abuse, and emotional neglect. Sadly, when asked about any sense of remorse, the participants believed that the crimes were bad only because they were caught—a sociopathic response. This characteristic of neglect was also found in a study by Harrington (1986). In a psychodynamic explanation of the incest perpetrator, Hirsch (1986) found that when the offender is the biological father, the daughter appears to take the place of the wife, an act accompanied by a suspension of reality. The father uses sex as a weapon of power and control. The mother is often aware of the abuse; Ringwalt et al. (1988) estimate that almost 70% of the wives know of the abuse and do nothing to stop it.

McIvor and Guthrie (1986) found no differences in MMPI scores between men who abused younger children and those who molested older children.

Rather than the age of the child, the biggest difference found in the psychology of the offenders may be geographical.

Low self-esteem is a common trait of incest perpetrators that appears in a great deal of the professional literature. Research shows, however, that there are also many other factors that can be considered either as causal or as correlates of incest: social isolation, unsatisfactory marital and sexual relationships, marital discord, role reversal, the wife's permission and/or collusion in the incest, the wife's being physically or psychologically ill, family dysfunction, alcoholism, and a seductive child (Cavaiola & Schiff, 1989; Salter, 1989). It is beyond the scope of this book to discuss the relative merits of the research that deals with the traits of incest offenders. However, it should be noted that most of the data suggest that the incest perpetrator is "made, and not born" (Wells, 1981).

Incestuous Behavior

The physical activity involved in incest when it involves a biological father or stepfather does not seem to differ, be it oral-genital or genital-genital contact (Groff & Hubble, 1984). In half of the cases, the sexual abuse is limited to fondling; in about one case in four, sexual intercourse or attempted sexual intercourse is present.

It appears that once the incest commences, the activity continues for about two years. According to Harrington (1986), most incest victims are between the ages of 8 and 12. In this age range children are most vulnerable, not only because they are so young, but because they are also becoming more independent and thus are less supervised.

The incest offender often promises love and affection to the victim, with a message, often stated, that the child is the most loved of all the children in the family. The incestuous activity is a "secret" shared only by the perpetrator and the victim, and no one will ever know about their special relationship.

The incestuous father usually spends an inordinate amount of time with the preferred victim. He may forbid his daughter to have friends of either sex, and especially boyfriends. In addition, he may show an inordinate amount of affection toward the victim. On other occasions, this offender may border on paranoia, thinking that the child-victim has been active with someone else or even reacting beyond reason if he suspects that the victim may have been molested by someone else (Salter, 1989, pp. 234-235).

Effects on the Child

Children who have been the victims of incest may indeed suffer lasting effects. One young woman, Rita C, who was molested by her mother and father from the time she was 9 until she was 16, told me in an interview that she was very sexually promiscuous. Rita said that the only way in which she felt she could gain personal acceptance with another person was to be sexual. The incest victim's developing sense of worthlessness is apparent in this poem, written by Beth, another victim (the poem is reproduced here by permission of the Louisville, Kentucky, chapter of Parents United):

Silence is my agony.
I dare not speak.
I close my eyes tightly.
I dare not flinch.

I calm my breathing.
I mustn't give away that I am awake.
You touch me under my blankets, and groan.
I feel vomit rise to my throat.

Now you take away my blanket and spread my legs.
My heart pounds wildly.
I cannot jump and run.
I feel your tongue on me and I feel faint.

I see stars.
I am going to DIE!
You are sucking the life out of me.
When you leave I can breathe again.

I get up and look into the mirror.
I see a monster.
It is me!
I want to DIE!
I can't live with the silence.
Why, why didn't I scream?
I strain to see the reason that I have caused all of this.
What is it about me that makes you act like this?
I am evil and I need to be destroyed!

There are also other effects on the child resulting from sexual abuse. Herman and Hirschman (1981) report that 33% of their sample of sexual abuse victims had run away from home during their teenage years; only 5% of their control sample had done so. In a study by Benward and Densen-Gerber (1975), 23% of the incest group had left home prior to age 14, compared with 11% of the nonincest group. By age 16, 52% of the incest group had left home, as opposed to 39% of the nonincest group. In a study I conducted for the Exploited and Missing Child Unit in Louisville, Kentucky, I found that there apparently exists a "career development ladder" among children who are victims of incest—prostitution and runaway behavior (Holmes, 1985). In this study of 267 children involved in the juvenile justice system, I found that 76% of the children who were involved in juvenile prostitution were also victims of incestuous families or victims of pedophiles.

Problems in relating to others, problems in the school and the community, mental health problems, and delinquency all are evidence of the very real dangers to children who are victims of sexual child abuse. But perhaps the greatest damage is the destruction of the child's self-perception. Many incest victims blame themselves, as the last stanza of Beth's poem shows.

CONCLUSION

The victimization of children has grown to such pandemic proportions in American society that each citizen should be vitally concerned with the ramifications of such acts. Children must not be viewed as objects to be used, abused, and discarded like broken toys. They are indeed the future of our society, and we, as concerned adults, must protect them from those who would do them harm.

5

Homosexuality

Most Americans view homosexuality as a sexual aberration. There are, of course, several reasons for this judgment; one that is most readily apparent is that of the religious norm that many believe homosexual practices violate. In the Old Testament, for example, Lot would have preferred that strangers sexually violate his daughters than his sons. The seed of man spilling upon the ground (condemned in the Old Testament), as in masturbation, is only one step removed from the same-sex practices of homosexuality. In neither case is procreation a possibility.

There are also other reasons some people are so violently opposed to homosexuality. Homosexuality is a personal as well as a religious affront to many. Now the added fear of the transmission of AIDS has reinforced homosexuals' placement in a category that many fear and wish to avoid. Of course, this is not always easy to accomplish—many persons who are homosexual are not easily recognizable; just as heterosexuals are not all the same, homosexuals form a varied population.

CATEGORIES OF HOMOSEXUALITY

Homosexual is a term derived from the Greek word *homos*, which means "the same." A form of sexuality and sexual orientation, homosexuality has existed since the start of recorded history. In both the Old and New Testaments, homosexuality is condemned. Punishments have been especially designed for those who practiced this form of sex, ranging from exile and incarceration in convents and seminaries to castration and various methods of execution.

Perhaps the study that did most to move homosexuality out of the darkness and into the consciousness of most Americans was the work of Alfred Kinsey. Kinsey, a world-famous zoologist, was beseeched by Dr. Herman Wells, the president of Indiana University, to coordinate a family studies course. The time was 1938. By the late 1940s, Kinsey, Weinberg, and others had established an international center for the scientific study of sexual behavior. Now called the Kinsey Sex Research Institute, these researchers published two books, *The Sexual Behavior of the Human Male* and *The Sexual Behavior of the Human Female*. Despite lacking sampling sophistication, Kinsey found, for example, that 37% of his white male population (remember the social climate of the time) had had at least one homosexual experience to the point of orgasm during their lifetimes. He also found that 13-17% of the female sample had had at least one lesbian experience. Other research has found that the statistics have not varied significantly since that time (Knox & Wilson, 1981; Marmor, 1980; Petersen, Kretchmer, Nellis, Lever, & Hertz, 1983).

THE GAY LIBERATION MOVEMENT

The gay liberation movement in the United States can be traced to the Stonewall Inn Riot in Greenwich Village in 1969 (see Table 5.1). A number of gays, complaining about police brutality and harassment of homosexuals in the city of New York, walled themselves inside the Stonewall Inn, a gay bar, and launched rocks and other missiles at the police barricaded outside. The riot marked the first time that homosexuals openly defied the police (and, some would say, society) and marked the beginnings of the gay population's coming out of the closet into the consciousness of American society.

TABLE 5.1. Important Dates in the Gay Liberation Movement

Date	Event
1948 and 1953	Kinsey's volumes on male and female homosexuality
1950s	finding of the Mattachine Society and Daughters of Bilitis
1969	Stonewall Inn Riot
Early 1970s	gay pride parades in New York and San Francisco
1973	founding of the national Gay Task Force
1975	Leonard Matlovich discharged from the Air Force as a result of his personal declaration of homosexuality
1977	successful revocation of the Dade County, Florida, ordinance prohibiting discrimination based on sexual orientation
1981	AIDS first reported
1986	Supreme Court upholds states' rights to restrain sodomy legally
1987 and 1989	marches on Washington and New York by militant gays

TYPES OF HOMOSEXUALS

Just as all people take part in varied social, business, and personal activities, being gay is only one part of a homosexual's daily life. Just as there are differences among heterosexuals, there are differences among homosexuals. In examining these differences it is important to have an understanding of some of the different categories of homosexuality. There are other typologies of homosexuality (see Table 5.2), but the following categories appear well defined for academic scrutiny and evaluation.

The Secret Homosexual

There is no valid method for ascertaining the total number of homosexuals in the United States today, partly because there are untold numbers who remain "in the closet" and never publicly acknowledge their sexual orientation. There appear to be two types of secret homosexuals. The first type includes persons who realize that they are gay but do not act out that sexuality. The second type includes those who recognize their homosexual tendencies and act out that sexual orientation, but keep the acts and behaviors secret from others.

TABLE 5.2. Typology of Gay Life-Styles

Category	Characteristics
Close-coupled	close personal and sexual relationships, less likely to seek outside partners (28% of lesbians and 10% of male homosexuals are in this category)
Open-coupled	lives with a primary partner but has outside sexual partners; reasons differ between sexes, but style appears less satisfying for females (17% of lesbians and 18% of male homosexuals are in this category)
Functional	single; report more sexual encounters; not interested in committed relationships (10% of lesbians and 15% of male homosexuals are in this category)
Dysfunctionals	dissatisfied with sexuality; more sexual problems. (5% of lesbians and 12% of male homosexuals are in this category)
Asexual	not involved with other gays; less interested in sex; fewer sexual partners (11% of lesbians and 16% of male homosexuals are in this category)

SOURCE: Adapted from Bell and Weinberg (1978).

A certain amount of paranoia may indeed be healthy for homosexuals trying to get along in a homophobic society. If one is a schoolteacher, bank president, officer of a large or small company, or government worker, or holds another type of sensitive position, one may be wise to conceal one's homosexuality. Secret homosexuals may prefer to keep their sexual orientation hidden rather than risk discovery and possible job loss and ostracism.

In Mansfield, Ohio, more than 20 years ago, the police carried out a sting operation during which they filmed men having sex in a public rest room. They then arrested several of the men, some of whom were prominent members of the Mansfield community. The film was publicly viewed and sold to various educational and training groups in the United States. This operation resulted in the suicide of several of the men who had been arrested. In Indianapolis, only recently, police arrested a man for operating a homosexual prostitution ring, and gathered from a computer the names of customers who had purchased the services of young men. In this instance also several men have committed suicide rather than undergo the shame of having their names made public.

The Adjusted Homosexual

Adjusted homosexuals are quite happy to be what they are. They accept their sexual orientation and thus do not suffer over their choices of sexual partners. They may face discrimination on the job, in housing, and so on, but this has little to do with sexual orientation per se.

Adjusted homosexuals may readily admit being gay when the issue arises, but, apart from this admission, they do not flaunt being homosexual. By all outward appearances, the adjusted homosexual appears no different from anyone else.

The Blatant Homosexual

Blatant homosexuals, through their actions, practically scream their gayness. The blatant homosexual's manner of speech, way of walking, mannerisms, and so on clearly exhibit his or her homosexuality. This person will typically frequent places where other homosexuals openly gather: gay bars, public rest rooms, public baths, parks. By going to these places, this person risks discovery and labeling, something that can be particularly devastating to a secret homosexual.

"Drag queens" (female impersonators) who work in gay bars may also be considered to be blatant homosexuals. This is not to say that all female impersonators are homosexuals, but it appears that the majority are gay. There are typically two reasons for someone to be a female impersonator. One, of course, is the money realized from working in this field of entertainment. The second is the opportunity to use the position as a manner in which to meet males for sexual encounters. Of course, the majority of these males would pay for sexual services.

The Institutional Homosexual

Institutional homosexuals typically do not view themselves as gay, even though they may have been involved in same-sex behaviors for several years while in situations that block access to the other sex. Typical examples are places such as the military, religious institutions (seminaries, convents), jails, and prisons.

The reason for homosexuality in men's prisons is fundamentally different from the reason this same activity occurs in women's prisons. Power appears to be a prime motivation for this action in men's prisons. When one prisoner sexually dominates and rapes another, the victim becomes the property of the dominant. This is graphically illustrated in the documentary *Scared Straight*, in which a prisoner sells a young male to another inmate for the price of a pack of cigarettes. The youngster becomes the "punk" of the inmate, not only for sexual purposes but also for housecleaning chores and anything else the inmate desired.

In women's prisons, homosexuality takes on an entirely different character. In talking with an inmate at a women's prison, I asked about the extent of lesbianism at the institution. She first stated that about three or four women there were involved with other women, but she was quick to add that this did not mean that there was any lesbian sexual activity occurring. She stated that since many of the women's husbands and boyfriends had abandoned them long ago, the relationships that developed inside the prison took the place of the families they left outside.

The Homosexual Prostitute

The ages of juvenile male homosexual prostitutes vary, with the mean and modal ages at 17 or 18 years; however, children as young as 7 years old are also involved in homosexual prostitution. The average age of the first prostitution experience is 14, but more active "dating" occurs a year or two later (Allen, 1980; Fisher, Weisberg, & Marotta, 1982).

Research has shown that the juvenile homosexual prostitute is typically from the lower social class; from a family where there is a great deal of discord, tension, and abuse; and from a home that is deprived and neglectful of the needs of the children. Many are from broken homes (Cory & LeRoy, 1963; MacNamara, 1965). Regardless of background, however, the homosexual prostitute engages in same-sex behavior for the same reasons that the older female prostitute engages in sex with her customers. Kinsey suggests that the number of young males involved in homosexual prostitution is no lower than the number of females in heterosexual prostitution (Kinsey, Pomeroy, & Martin, 1948, p. 596). Coleman (1989) suggests that male juvenile prostitutes suffer from some type of faulty social and personality development that makes them vulnerable to the situational variables that they encounter.

TABLE 5.3. Typology of Gay Life-Styles

Crime	Characteristics
Murder	committed by "pickups" or "tricks" persons who hate gays, or lovers or other homosexuals during angry arguments
"Fag Bashing"	committed by persons who hate homosexuals (includes beating and sometimes robbing them); many of these incidents in the past not reported to the police
"Gacy-style" murders	serial murder of homosexuals (named for John Gacy who slew 33 young males in the Chicago area after homosexually assaulting them; Gacy is awaiting execution in Chester, Illinois)
Assaults, battery, knifing, and disorderly conduct	result from lovers' quarrels and fights between homosexuals

SOURCE: Adapted from Gardner (1989, p. 482).

More than a few cities have well-organized juvenile prostitution rings, with adults pimping for the children. Kerry Rice, a professor of social work at the University of Louisville, believes that many rings do indeed exist, but they are not of the kind that many people believe. Professor Rice (personal communication, 1984) has stated that many young people pass the word around very quickly when a pedophile is willing to spend money on quick sex. This point of view is shared by John B, an incarcerated pedophile who told me that it was amazing that on every payday, several homosexual prostitutes were at his door to see if he wanted a "date."

The Homosexual Pedophile

As stated in Chapter 4, the adult sexual orientation of the pedophile should not be confused with the sex of the child he desires to have sex with. The homosexual pedophile, however, is a homosexual who desires to have sex only with same-sex children. It must be stressed, however, that the majority of homosexuals are not involved with children, nor do they wish to be so involved. They share the same sense of abhorrence as the rest of society when a child is molested, either inside or outside the family.

The homosexual pedophile is a "child lover" (as explained in Chapter 4), and is interested only in a same-sex child. Despised by society, this perpetrator is treated most harshly by the criminal justice system.

HOMOSEXUALITY AND THE LAW

Historically, not all societies have condemned homosexuality. In Mexico, for example, it was once quite accepted, as it was also among some Native American tribes (Carrier, 1989). This same statement cannot be made about the mainstream United States (Storms, 1978), of course.

Attitudes in U.S. society today reflect hostility directed against gays (see Table 5.3 for examples of crimes committed against homosexuals). Across the United States, sodomy laws have been passed. Police typically do not enforce these laws unless one of the actors is a juvenile and the other an adult, but there are also other laws that regulate homosexual activities.

Sodomy laws usually contain wording regarding same-sex physical activity as well as prescribed penalties. *Bowers v. Hardwick* in Georgia dramatically illustrates the hostile attitude of society toward homosexuality. Hardwick, a homosexual, was arrested by a police officer who had come to Hardwick's home to serve a legal paper. Looking through the front door, the officer observed Hardwick performing oral sex upon another man and arrested him. Hardwick was charged with oral sodomy and found guilty. The case was appealed all the way to the U.S. Supreme Court, which ruled that states can make laws to restrain same-sex activity.

Of course, not all legal organizations agree with the Supreme Court's decision. For example, the American Law Institute encourages the abolition of all laws concerning adults who are involved in consensual sex acts. The American Psychological Association argues for constitutional protection for consensual sodomy. Regardless of these stances, the law remains very punitive against homosexuals. Sentences for illegal same-sex activity range from three years to life; the average sentence handed down is three years (Cameron, 1988).

ETIOLOGY OF HOMOSEXUALITY

There are various explanations that attempt to pinpoint the etiology of homosexuality. Typically, these explanations center on the idea that something has gone terribly wrong, or else the person would be heterosexual. Why a person is heterosexual is seldom questioned. Therefore, built into all the theories is the assumption that something is abnormal, either physically (homosexuals are that way because of "incorrect" hormones or personal chemistry) or psychologically (homosexuals are that way because they have experienced faulty learning processes).

Biological Theories

Money (1980) reports little evidence that homosexuality is strictly an inborn trait. Kallman (1952a, 1952b) studied identical twins and found that, 100% of the time, if one twin was homosexual, the other was also. However, Kallman's sampling technique was faulty, and it would be a mistake to make generalized statements from this study. Heston and Shields (1968) could not find in their sample any data that would validate Kallman's findings.

Other research has pointed toward some form of hormonal imbalance as an explanation for homosexuality. For example, Murphy and Fain (1978) conclude that prenatal hormone imbalances can alter both masculine and feminine development in the brain of the fetus, and the result could be homosexuality. Bell, Weinberg, and Hammersmith (1981) state that homosexuality "is a pattern of feelings and reactions within the child that cannot be traced back to a single social or psychological root" (p. 192) and that "a boy or a girl is predisposed to be homosexual or heterosexual, and during childhood and adolescence this basic sexual orientation begins to become evident" (p. 187).

Other researchers have studied hormone levels in adults, but their results have not been consistent (Meyer-Bahlburg, 1977; Tourney, 1980). Regardless, it does not appear that there is any great body of knowledge that does more than strongly suggest that there is a relationship between homosexuality and biology.

Psychological Theories

Perhaps one of the most popular beliefs regarding the etiology of homosexuality lies within the theoretical construct of an unresolved Oedipus complex. Freud suggested years ago that a male would be homosexual if the Oedipus complex (in the case of a young girl, the Electra complex) was not satisfactorily resolved. Freud believed that a psychologically or physically lacking father plays a pivotal role in the etiology of homosexuality. Lacking in empirical validation, this stance still has some popularity. However, not everyone agrees with this position. Many believe that the role of the parents has been grossly exaggerated, and that no single factor can be identified that might cause an individual to be either homosexual or heterosexual.

Bieber et al. (1962) found passive or absent fathers in the family backgrounds of many gay males. In a sample of homosexual males with one absent parent, Saghir and Robins (1973) found that the mother was overcontrolling or the father was emotionally distant. However, Bell et al. (1981) believe that the role of the father or of the mother has been greatly exaggerated and has little influence upon the sexuality of the child.

In many theories of psychological development regarding homosexuality, it appears that homosexuality is viewed as some type of passing sexual orientation. Since this is the case, it is assumed that therapy can change someone from homosexual to heterosexual. This posture raises several issues, among them, whether or not sexual orientation can indeed be changed. Can someone who is a functioning sexual being be changed through therapy into a sexual being with diametrically opposed sexual desires and behaviors? This is the issue that must be addressed within many traditional therapies. It may be a far better approach—rather than working on a "cure"—to help homosexuals cope with living in a world that directs such a degree of hostility against them.

HOMOSEXUALITY AND
THE CRIMINAL JUSTICE SYSTEM

There is little empirical evidence demonstrating that homosexuals are overrepresented in arrests or in the courts. However, in only a few states—Illinois and Connecticut, for example—is homosexuality not considered to be a crime. A great deal of shame, disgrace, and public ridicule are heaped on a person arrested, much less convicted, on charges of homosexuality; often the experience is worse than for those arrested and convicted of armed robbery, assault, or even murder. Even in cases of child molestation, if the offender is gay he is labeled even more negatively than he would be if he were heterosexual.

It is often asserted that police routinely harass gays and lesbians (Barlow, 1990, p. 375). The case in Ohio mentioned above as well as arrests made in public rest rooms and in public parks where gays often gather are ready evidence that the criminal justice system has a different standard when gays are involved. Barlow (1990) states that most of the gays who are arrested, other than gay prostitutes and homosexual pedophiles, are first-time offenders and are arrested for misdemeanors. They are unsophisticated in the workings of the criminal justice system and are easy prey for unscrupulous police officers, attorneys, and public officials. Targets for extortion and blackmail, they are easily victimized.

CONCLUSION

There is some hope that a more tolerant attitude is emerging in the United States toward acts between consenting adults. Sodomy laws are for the most part currently not being enforced, unless there is force used or the victim is a minor. The National Crime Survey ranks consensual acts of homosexuality fourteenth from the bottom of 204 crimes. However, the advent of AIDS, which many people mistakenly refer to as the "gay disease," may serve as a force that will once again harden attitudes against all homosexuals.

6

Dangerous Sex Crimes

There are a multitude of sex crimes that are dangerous to societal members as well as to the individual practitioners themselves. Necrophilia, lust murder, anthropophagy, autoeroticism, pyromania, and serial murder are such crimes. These crimes are responsible for the victimization and death of untold numbers of people year in and year out.

The purpose of this chapter is to examine these particular types of sex crimes and how they affect people, especially women, in our society. Sex offenders themselves are also examined. The directions in which society is moving regarding the dangerous sex criminal are briefly discussed (Chapter 10 offers more extensive discussion of treatment for sex offenders).

NECROPHILIA

Once thought to be especially rare and a male perversion only (A. Ellis, 1986), necrophilia is now being seen more and more often. Historically, the use of dead bodies as vaults of sexual desire has been well documented (Brill, 1941). Burg (1982) disagrees with the assumption that necrophilia is rare, arguing that many cases are simply not discovered or reported. A number of incidents of necrophilia are currently being investigated.

Bartholomew, Milte, and Galbally (1978) report two cases of necrophilia. One case was that of a 22-year-old male who had homosexual tendencies that varied in intensity over the years. He carried out his fantasy of taking a male friend into the mountains, shooting him in the head, and then sexually molesting the corpse. The other case concerned a 47-year-old single male who sodomized a 9-year-old boy and then killed him with a blow to the head. He then returned to the body after several hours and sodomized the boy again. Freire Arteta (1981) presents a case of a 28-year-old female who had sexual relations with a corpse, and Foerster, Foerster, and Roth (1976) relate a similar story concerning a 17-year-old. When I interviewed a serial murderer on San Quentin's death row, he admitted to me that he had cut the heads off of several prostitutes and that he and his accomplice, a female, performed sexual acts with these heads.

As with any sex crime, fantasy plays an important role in the necrophiliac's actions (Baker, 1983). Because this appears to be the case, Goldenson (1970) reports that funerals, cemeteries, morgues, and autopsies hold great interest for necrophiliacs. DSM-III-R describes necrophilia as an atypical paraphilia and defines it as having sexual intercourse with a corpse (American Psychiatric Association, 1987). However, this definition is too limited. There is more to necrophilia than having intercourse with a dead body. As a deputy coroner, I have seen bodies that have been sexually assaulted after death and have talked with sex criminals who have robbed graves to have sex with corpses. A syndicated columnist often repeats a letter that she received from a woman whose husband demanded that she take a cold shower, douse herself with powder, and lie completely still in bed while he had intercourse with her. If she moved in response to his advances, he lost his ability to perform sexually. Certainly this man has a fantasy that centers on sex with a dead person, a form of necrophilia.

Levels of Necrophilia

There are at least three types of necrophiliacs. The first type is similar to the husband described above. This person "only" fantasizes about having sex with a corpse. His partner is alive but, in a cooperative sex relationship, pretends to be dead. A prostitute I spoke with stated that she had two clients with this type of "trip." She said that both men were professional types, one a lawyer and the other a dean of a local university, who were frequent customers; the attorney only wanted to look at her while she lay on the bed, while the latter customer would have intercourse with her.

The second type of necrophiliac is a person who has sex with a person who is already dead. This person will sometimes place him- or herself in an occupational role where he or she has access to dead bodies: morgue attendant, funeral home personnel, coroner. Often a disorganized offender (Ressler, 1986a), this paraphiliac gains easy access to corpses, so the fantasy that demands sexual activity with a corpse can be easily realized.

The third type of necrophile is the necrosadistic offender. This person murders to have sex with a dead body. There are many examples of this type, including Ted Bundy (see Chapter 1), Albert Fish, and Ed Gein. In this form, as well as the second type, necrophilia must be viewed as the ultimate and most extreme form of erotic eligibility distancing—that is, the partner must be dead (Money, 1984).

A similar typology has been developed by Rosman and Resnick (1989) (see Table 6.1). The pseudonecrophiliac has a transient attraction to corpses and, although the fantasy includes having sex with a person just killed, corpses are not the object of the sexual fantasy—living partners are preferred. The second type is the genuine necrophiliac, and this is divided into three subtypes: the homicidal necrophiliac, who murders to have sex with a dead body; the regular necrophiliac, who uses already-dead bodies for sexual pleasure; and the necrophilic fantasy offender, who merely fantasizes about having sex with the dead. Rosman and Resnick studied 122 necrophiles and found that the sex of the corpse desired mirrored the sexual orientation of the necrophile. Some 79% were heterosexual, 64% had histories of prior sadistic sexual acts, 86% had nonnecrophilic intercourse, over half were diagnosed with personality disorders, 17% were psychotic, and most were of above-average intelligence. The subjects in this research gathered their bodies through their work: hospital orderly, cemetery employee, morgue attendant, funeral parlor assistant, soldier, cleric, pathologist, anatomy student, and ambulance driver. Only a few committed homicide; the majority simply took advantage of chance opportunities.

Etiology of Necrophilia

No one knows the precise etiology of necrophilia. Since there are widespread differences among types of necrophiliacs, from those who merely fantasize to those who kill, explanations will certainly vary. Calef and Weinshel (1972) and Faguet (1980) state that the fantasies that accompany

TABLE 6.1. Typology of Necrophiles

Category	Characteristics
Pseudo necrophile	transient attraction to a corpse, but living partners are the preferred choice
Homicidal necrophile	murders to have sex with the dead (the necrosadistic sex offender)
Regular necrophile	uses already dead bodies for sex (may work where there are already bodies—morgues, cemetaries, etc.)

SOURCE: Adapted from Rosman and Resnick (1989).

the necrophilic act express a desire to reenter and explore the maternal body. Further elaborating, according to this view, the necrophiliac desires also to replace a rival fetus and to replace the paternal phallus. Other psychodynamic considerations may lie in the areas of a neurotic mother fixation, preoccupation with the mother's death, alcohol abuse, and social personality deprivation (Janik & Chromy, 1979). Of course, it would be most difficult to validate this theory.

H. Ellis (1946) has reported that necrophiliacs are often feebleminded or possess a high degree of psychopathology (Katchadourian & Lunde, 1975). Of course, this is not always true. Lancaster (1978) reports the case of a male with an IQ of 153 and with no signs of psychopathology reported prior to the incident. This necrophiliac broke into a mortuary on two separate occasions to have sexual intercourse with a corpse but was unsuccessful each time. Deciding to obtain a corpse by his own hand, this sex offender then broke into a home, where he stabbed a woman to death and had sexual intercourse with her.

Many necrophiliacs are insensitive to others and have a great hatred for women. The mutilation that occurs to the dead body of the female reduces the worth of the corpse and increases the emotional excitement of the act itself. Because the victim is dead—in the case of the necrosadistic offender and the one who has sex with corpses—the sex criminal does not risk rejection; the helplessness of the corpse could certainly enter into the decision to assault the body sexually (Holmes, 1983; Weeks, 1986).

INFIBULATION

Infibulation, an inward-directed dangerous sex crime, is torture of one's own body. This sex act is masochistic; often it involves piercing the flesh of one's own genitals. Albert Fish, a serial killer and mysoped in New York in the early twentieth century, was an infibulator. After he was electrocuted in New York's electric chair, the autopsy showed that he had more than two dozen sewing needles inserted into his scrotum and penis.

Tattooing is viewed by some as one form of infibulation. Tattooing is an art form of body adornment developed in Japan and Polynesia. Among men of the lower social classes in the United States, tattoos serve as symbols of masculinity and toughness. In some other cultures, cicatrization (scarification) is held to be absolutely necessary to manhood (Ellis & Abarbanel, 1967).

In some Third World countries, as many as 90% of females are circumcised to inhibit sex urges and to reduce clitoral growth (Ebomoyi, 1987). Of course, this form of infibulation, like tattooing, has little to do with sexual masochism.

Other forms of infibulation include the insertion of rings into the nipples, labia, clitoris, or penis. In one case, a 28-year-old female admitted repeatedly to a psychiatric hospital for acute depression was evaluated because of her insertion into her urethra of an injectable razor blade that then lodged in her bladder. The patient had done this on numerous occasions when she felt lonely and "needed to feel alive." In another case, a 47-year-old man admitted to masturbating intraurethrally with a thin wooden stick. While masturbating, he fantasized about being a woman having sexual intercourse with a man (Wise, 1982).

Etiology of the Infibulator

This form of sexual abuse has not received the serious research study that many other forms of behavior have. One study, however, lists six etiological factors in the background of the infibulator: abuse by relatives as a child, long and intense sexual confusion, masochistic relations with and submission to women, strong female identification, penis repudiation, and depression that is relieved by mutilation (Bourgeois, 1983). Conacher and Westwood (1987) believe that infibulators are often not paranoid schizophrenics—a point not accepted by Hall, Lawson, and Wilson (1981) or Silva, Leong, and

Weinstock (1989)—but that they have a deeply hidden doubt about their sexual identity and a previous history of self-abuse. Another reason may include an urge to rid oneself of unacceptable sexual urges that are viewed as dirty and evil (Fisch, 1987; Greenberg et al., 1989b). It may be that a combination of biological, psychological, and social factors, as well as the culture in which the person is reared, account for a propensity for infibulation (Favazza, 1989).

AUTOEROTICISM

The term *autoeroticism* means involvement in a sexual behavior without a partner. There are several types of autoeroticism, including masturbation, erotic asphyxiation, and aquaeroticism. Simple masturbation poses no danger to the person who practices it. Despite the claims made years ago regarding "self-abuse," there is no evidence of any relationship between masturbation and physical injury. Erotic hanging and aquaeroticism are quite a different story, however.

Erotic Asphyxiation

This solitary sex act is practiced predominantly but not exclusively by males. As many as 1,000 accidental deaths a year may be attributed to erotic asphyxiation (Burgess & Hazelwood, 1983; Milner, 1981). The person involved in this form of sex typically uses some type of mechanism to impede the flow of oxygen to the brain in order to heighten sexual pleasure. This oxygen deficiency somehow enhances feelings of sexual excitement (although there is no clear understanding of how this works). The enhancement mechanism can be a ligature, a plastic bag, or an inhalant such as gas or a chemical aerosol (Lowery & Wetli, 1982; Polson & Gee, 1973, p. 473). A rope is the most common method used to induce asphyxia. Luke (1967) reports that many men and women use some type of padding (towels, scarves, sweaters) under the ligature to prevent abrasions on the neck when a rope is used.

Often, deaths resulting from erotic asphyxia are misclassified. For example, a young person is found hanged from a tree in a public park, nude, with clothing neatly folded near the tree. It may well be that the young person committed suicide, but it is also possible the person was involved in erotic hanging and the release mechanism malfunctioned. In one recent reported case, the manager of a department was found hanging from a rafter in his

TABLE 6.2. Typical Elements in Erotic Hanging

Practiced by adolescent or young adult

Ropes, belts, or other binding material that can be controlled
    by the practitioner

Evidence of masturbation

Partial or complete nudity

Solitary and compulsive act

No apparent wish to die

Presence of pornography

Cross-dressing in males

Repetitive act

---

office at a construction site. He was nude except for a semen guard (which is common among practitioners of erotic asphyxia), and his hands and feet were tied. In front of him was a collection of pornography that aided in his fantasy. In examining his personal effects, his mother found magazines and letters that he had written to members of the Olenspeigel Society, a national organization for erotic asphyxiates. This was a classic case, and of course there was no misclassification. (For a list of typical elements found in erotic hanging, see Table 6.2.)

Sheehan and Garfinkel (1988) studied nine young male paraphiliacs who had died as a result of erotic hanging. These researchers identified some common features of erotic asphyxiation, including the presence of partial or total undress, cross-dressing, the presence of pornographic material, evidence of penile enlargement, and some form of bondage. There is obviously a lack of a suicide note, because this is a sex act and not a suicide attempt.

Further examples illustrate these common elements. In one case, on arriving at work one morning the owner of a gay bar found the bar manager (a male) dead in the women's rest room. The manager was lying on the floor, dressed in a woman's slip. There was an opened newspaper on the floor in front of him and an amount of semen on the floor. The rope around his neck had not slipped as designed, and he had died of asphyxia. Cesnik and Coleman (1989) report the case of a 24-year-old male who sought treatment for depression; his ritualized and compulsive autoerotic behavior included putting plastic bags over his head, binding his head with duct tape, tying himself up, and wearing a diving suit.

Characteristics of Erotic Asphyxiates

Lowery and Wetli (1982) report that the overwhelming majority of those involved in erotic asphyxia are young, white, middle-class, unmarried males. Saunders (1989) found that of 43 persons who had died by autoerotic asphyxia, 35 were men under the age of 30 (the age range was 14-75), two-thirds were single, and most were white. One in three practiced transvestism.

Because few persons will openly admit to the practice of erotic asphyxiation, the characteristics of those who indulge in these acts are gleaned from those who have failed in their practice—that is, from those who have died. Haydn-Smith, Marks, and Repper (1989, p. 518) report that they found in their study characteristics of youth, transvestism, and masturbation; most practitioners are male, and only a few seek help. Burgess and Hazelwood (1983, p. 166), in a study of 132 cases of erotic asphyxiates, found that 96% were males, 65% were less than 30 years of age, 94% were white, and almost 60% were single.

Aquaerotic Asphyxiation

In a case reported in a southern state, a man came home from work in the afternoon to find his 21-year-old wife dead. She was dressed in a jogging suit, with a heavy knit tie around her neck, and her hands were bound in front of her. Her face was in three inches of water; she had drowned. Upon interrogation, the husband admitted that his wife had been involved in erotic hanging. She had usually practiced this form of solitary sex in the bathroom, a fact that was verified by various rope burns on the top of the bathroom door. Apparently, she had tried to induce partial drowning to enhance sexual excitement. The results were fatal.

Sivaloganathan (1984) describes aquaeroticum (autoerotic drowning) in the case of a 36-year-old male who was found at the bottom of a river encased in a bag. His wrists and ankles were tied loosely together, and his right forefinger was passed through the small loop of a pair of scissors. Upon investigation it was determined that the man was practicing aquaeroticism and apparently had accidentally drowned before he could cut himself free.

This form of autoeroticism appears to be very rare, but the elements in the practice are not too different from those found in erotic asphyxiation: a complicated use of ligatures involving the genitals and neck, pornography, and so on.

Summary

Forms of autoerotic behavior other than those discussed above have been recorded as well. In 1981, for example, Sivaloganathan reported the cases of devotees involved in the practice of insertion of objects—lamps, electrical cords—in their bodily orifices that resulted in fatal electrocutions. Although some forms of autoerotic behavior are potentially lethal, there is little known about the characteristics of persons who become involved in this form of sexual activity. Additional research needs to be done in this area.

Because there is such a dearth of information, there is a great need for social action programs designed to inform the public as well as practitioners of these potentially dangerous sexual acts. There must be an added effort to inform mental health professionals of the growing numbers of persons involved in this paraphilia and of methods developed to enable them to deal with this form of sexual activity.

PYROMANIA

There are approximately 20,000 incidents of arson per year in the United States. There are many types of arson (see Table 6.3). Fire setting for revenge or for commercial purposes are two forms of arson. Pyromania is yet another. Pyromania is an eroticized form of arson. It is a pathological condition characterized by a compulsive factor that becomes very strong, until there is an inability to refrain from this behavior. Masters and Roberson (1990, p. 308) estimate that about 40% of fire setters are pyromaniacs, although that is a statistic that some feel may be too high.

Pyromaniacs commit arson, but their motivation is different from that of other types of fire setters; theirs is an erotic motive. In some instances, the pyromaniac ignites a fetish (e.g., shoes, panties), and, although the fire is initially specific in character, it may spread to an entire building (Haas & Haas, 1990), sometimes resulting in the deaths of innocent people.

As with many sex offenders, there appears to be a situational impulse that sets the pyromaniac into action. Bourget and Bradford (1987) relate the case of one young adult as follows: As a child he was fascinated with fire, but his first experience of arson occurred when he was a young adult. He went into a bar, felt rejected and angry when he was not able to meet anyone, and left the bar to set a fire. This became a pattern of fire-setting behavior in his residential neighborhood. His fire setting involved both

TABLE 6.3. Types of Arson

Type	Characteristics
Organized crime	loan sharking, extortion, strippers, and other crime concealments
Insurance and housing fraud	overinsurance, blockbusting, parcel clearance
Commercial	inventory depletion, stop loss, and modernization
Residential	public housing, relocation, automobile, and redecorating

SOURCE: Macy (1979).

an erotic component and a typical motive of revenge. When he was unsuccessful with females, he abused alcohol, only to become more angry and resentful. In this state of mind he would set a fire. He would see images of women in the fire and become sexually aroused. He would then masturbate, watching the fire. Then he would go home and masturbate again while reading pornography. As the behavior continued, it led to erotic feelings of power and sexual arousal.

The pyromaniac experiences sexual excitement at the sight of a fire or smoke, and this leads to urination, erection, masturbation, and/or spontaneous orgasm. This sex offender often sets a fire and then stands apart and watches not only the fire but the calamity the fire has produced (Money, 1985).

Characteristics of the Pyromaniac

McCary (1978, p. 357) states that pyromania affects only males. This point is contested slightly by the research of Crossley and Guzman (1985), who state that the pyromaniac is "primarily a male." Karpman (1957) also disagrees with this position. According to Karpman, sometimes the pyromaniac is not only a female, but she will set fires "either prior to or during menstruation or during pregnancy" (p. 140). This sex offender is typically young and experiences sexual frustration and tension that commences with a feeling of compulsion to start a fire.

There appear to be some common characteristics that the majority of known pyromaniacs possess. For example, many suffered physical child abuse, poor parental relationships, and severe conduct disorders

(Lowenstein, 1989). Oliver (1974) believes that many pyromaniacs are mentally retarded, severely paranoid, schizophrenic, alcoholic, or sexually sadistic.

Summary

Pyromania, while sexually motivated, is a very dangerous sexual practice because of the real peril it presents to unaware citizens. Treatment programs directed toward this type of arsonist must be expanded if the statistics that have been reported are at least remotely accurate.

LUST MURDER

Holmes and De Burger (1985; see also Holmes, 1989) have developed a typology of serial murderers that includes visionary, mission, hedonistic, and power/control types. The visionary and mission types kill typically not for sexual purposes. However, the hedonistic types (of which there are two subtypes, *lust* and *thrill*) and power/control killers certainly are impelled by sex to kill. John Gacy, Ted Bundy, Douglas Clark, Ottis Toole, Gerald Stano, Carol Bundy, Kenneth Bianchi, and Angelo Buono are all examples of this type of extremely dangerous offender.

The Lust Killer

The lust-type serial killer is one who has made a vital connection between sexual gratification and fatal violence. This type of serial killer is motivated by the hunger for sexual gratification. Unfortunately, many such killers are sadistic to the extent that their sexual pleasure depends on the amount of torture and mutilation they can administer, and ultimately on the killing of their victims. These killers are typically in touch with reality and can establish relationships with other persons, but their sexual gratification comes from the use and the abuse of people they view as sexual objects.

Elaborate stalking, carefully planned activities regarding the extermination of the victim, and sexual experimentation after death (necrophilia) are often elements in lust killings; mutilation of the victim is often perpetrated as well. Jerry Brudos, a serial killer from Oregon, was such a killer. Lust killers often select women and children as victims, and many seek an ideal victim type. Killing by strangulation and skin to skin contact are common. Often diagnosed as an antisocial personality, this killer represents a very real danger to society. Consider the following from an interview I conducted with a serialist who is currently in prison for the murder of several young women.

Almost seventeen years have passed since the little blonde named Becky died alone in the darkness of my bedroom closet. And perhaps more appalling than the raw brutality surrounding her demise is that she was not my only victim that fateful day. Less than two hours after Becky's life had ended, there was yet another, slightly older girl laying naked and bound inside my bedroom. This second girl's name is long forgotten now, but it was she who was forced to endure all of the sadistic cruelties that I'd failed to carry out on her dead predecessor. While she lay tied down to my bed, I terrorized and battered and tortured this girl for more than an hour, covering up the sound of her gag-muffled screams with music from a loudly blaring radio. Next, after becoming intensely aroused by the sight and sound of her agony, I lowered myself onto the bed and started raping her, continuing with this assault until I wanted her no more. Finally, then, having no further need of this second victim, I wrapped an extension cord around her neck and pulled hard on the ends, strangling her until I was certain that she, like the blond-headed Becky before her, was dead.

So began my career as a killer. I had only recently celebrated by twentieth birthday when these, my first two murders, were carried out inside my home. Several years would pass and I'd be just under 24 before capture and imprisonment finally put an end to my habit of killing. Throughout the years in between, however, I would succeed at luring a multitude of unsuspecting young women into the front seat of my car and on into the house where I lived. Most of these young females were hitchhikers, some were stranded motorists whose cars had broken down along uncrowded highways, and others were lone pedestrians who were just naive or incautious enough to follow me to the moon on the promise of a free high. And, in almost every instance, I ended up torturing and raping and murdering these young women, filling their last hours with pain and agony.

The lust killer often combines aberrant sexual practices, including picquerism, flagellation, anthropophagy, and necrosadistic acts. Picquerism is the intense desired to stab, wound, or cut the flesh of another person. Walter Kehlback, currently in prison in Utah, has admitted liking to see people suffer. He says that he likes to cut people, and knifing someone is like cutting through foam rubber. Often these stab wounds are inflicted near the genitals or breasts in a lust killing (DeRiver, 1956).

Flagellationism is an intense desire to beat, whip, or club someone. This form of sadism often leads to victims being severely beaten and sexually abused. A careful examination of the scene of such a crime might yield a find of semen that resulted from flagellationism.

Vampirism is rare, but it does occur. I recently completed a profile for a police department in a southern state in which eight young women were found, all nude, with no blood left in their bodies. There were puncture wounds found in the left arm of each victim. Immediately, the police suspected some type of occult group operating in the area. There were no other forms of abuse, victims had not been sexually abused, and there were no signs of satanic involvement (burn marks, tattoos, or the like). The profile suggested that the evidence indicated a sex criminal with a propensity for vampirism. The police finally arrested an engineer who had abducted nine women, tying each to his kitchen table and draining her blood. He kept the blood in mason jars in his refrigerator to drink when he wanted it. The ninth victim managed to loosen her bonds after he went to work; she escaped and went to the police.

John Haigh killed nine women in 1949. After killing one victim, Haigh remarked:

> I shot her in the back of the head. Then I went out to the car and fetched a drinking glass and made an incision, I think with a penknife, in the side of the throat and collected a glass of blood which I then drank. (Blundell, 1983, p. 74)

Ted Bundy admitted to having feelings of vampirism. He also, on at least one occasion, bit off the nipple of one victim and ingested it.

Cannibalism, or anthropophagy, appears to be more common than vampirism. Jack the Ripper, for example, was said to have sent one kidney of one of his victims to Scotland Yard, with a note saying that he had eaten the other (Chesser, 1971; Shuster, 1975). Fritz Haarman kidnapped, murdered, butchered, and stored the remains of young boys. Only recently, Gary Heidnik was arrested in Philadelphia with the body parts of one victim cooking on his kitchen range. Ed Gein, Albert Fish, and other lust killers are also examples of cannibals.

Sometimes anthropophagy is inner-directed. Stoller (1985) reports one patient who, after failing in relationships with women, would eat parts of his own flesh. Each time he ate his own skin, he discovered that he received pleasurable orgasms.

Characteristics of the Lust Killer

Ressler, Burgess, and Douglas (1988) report that fantasy plays an important role in the murderous acts of the lust killer. Many of these killers come

TABLE 6.4. Traits of the Organized Lust Killer

Personal Characteristics	Postoffense Behavior
High intelligence	Returns to crime scene
Socially adequate	Volunteers information
Sexually competent	Police "groupie"
Lives with partner	Anticipates questioning
High birth-order status	May move body
Harsh discipline	May dispose body to advertise crime
Controlled mood during crime	
Masculine image	
Charming, charismatic	
Situational to crime	
Geographically mobile	
Occupationally mobile	
Follows media	
Model prisoner	

SOURCE: FBI Law Enforcement Bulletin, 1985.
NOTE: Interview techniques useful with this kind of offender include a direct strategy and certainty about details. These offenders will admit to only what they must.

from homes where there was a great deal of physical, sexual, and emotional abuse.

It has been hypothesized that lust killers who have "organized" personalities are generally of above-average intelligence, are socially competent, plan their killings, and move the bodies of their victims so that the crime scene is usually different from the place where the body was found. If the lust killer's personality is of a disorganized character, the opposite characteristics appear to be true ("Crime Scene and Profile Characteristics," 1985, pp. 18-20) (see Tables 6.4 and 6.5). Revitch and Schlesinger (1989) add another item to the traits of the lust killer from a psychodynamic perspective: displaced anger toward females, originally directed toward the killer's mother.

It is important to avoid confusing causes of lust killing with the characteristics of some lust killers. One expert in the area of serial murder has developed a list of "traits of serial killers": white, male, intelligent, travels continually in his search for victims, and so on. These are not causes, but they are indeed traits of some serial lust killers. However, there are so many exceptions that such a list becomes almost meaningless. The situation is that

TABLE 6.5. Traits of the Disorganized Lust Killer

Personal Characteristics	Postoffense Behavior
Below-average intelligence	Returns to crime scene
Socially inadequate	May attend funeral/burial
Unskilled work	May place memoria in media
Low birth-order status	May turn to religion
Father's work unstable	May keep diary
Anxious mood during crime	May change job
Minimal use of alcohol	May have personality change
Lives alone	
Lives/works near crime	
Minimal interest in media	
Significant behavioral change	
Nocturnal	
Secret hiding places	
Usually does not date	
High school dropout	

Source: FBI Law Enforcement Bulletin, 1985.
NOTE: Interview techniques useful with this kind of offender include using a counselor approach; emphathizing; and introducing evidence indirectly. Nighttime interviews may be most productive.

lust killers are real and present dangers. Furthermore, there is no real protection against these persons. (I realize that this is an unpopular view; I once made this statement on *Donohue*, and it was not well received.)

CONCLUSION

This chapter has focused upon very dangerous sex offenders. The reader will notice that, while sadism and masochism have not been explored directly as distinct topics, sex behaviors that inflict pain and suffering upon hapless and helpless victims are an integral part of dangerous sex crimes. Every year, thousands of victims are targets of offenders who commit the crimes discussed in this chapter. New names are continually coming to our attention—Gary Heidnik, Gerald Gallego, John Story, Cameron Hooker, Randy Craft—graphically illustrating that victimization is not declining.

7

Rape

It is commonly agreed that rape is a crime of violence. It affects more than a million women a year in the United States (Masters & Roberson, 1990, p. 379). Koss, Gidycz, and Wisniewski (1987) sampled more than 6,000 American college students regarding their sexual experiences and found that 27.5% of the college women reported they had been raped since the age of 14, and 7.7% of the men reported perpetrating rape. In Estrich's (1987) study of women on college campuses, 20% of the women reported having been "physically forced" to have sexual intercourse. Similar results were found by Warshaw (1988): In Warshaw's sample, 25% of the women had experienced rape or attempted rape; 84% of the victims were acquainted with their assailants; 5% had reported their rapes to the police; 27% of rape victims had identified themselves as such; and 1 in 12 men admitted to committing acts that meet the legal definition of rape. The statistics resulting from such surveys may be more accurate than those from law enforcement and criminal justice records in depicting the full extent of sexual victimization, because many victims and perpetrators are never involved in the criminal justice system (Koss et al., 1987).

Exhibit 7.1

Rape Statistics Show . . .

Rapists usually have raped approximately 14 times for each time they are caught.

Rapists are on an ascending scale of violence with each assault.

More than 50% of all rapes occur in the home of the victim.

More than 93% of the time, the assailant and the victim are of the same race.

SOURCE: Rape Relief Center, Louisville, KY (1990).

The mass media constantly represent males in superior social and physical positions and women as helpless and vulnerable. In films, for example, women are often depicted not only as vulnerable victims, but as victims who, once raped, degraded, and dehumanized, come to accept this treatment and to "grow to love" their attackers (Wilson, 1988). *Tie Me Up, Tie Me Down* and *9 ½ Weeks* are examples of recent films that show men dehumanizing women who then fall madly in love with them.

Rape carries with it beliefs that legitimate this violent behavior. Consider, for example, some common images of male-female relationships, as summarized by Brownmiller (1975) and Russell (1983):

(1) the assumption of male dominance and female vulnerability

(2) the idea that a woman's body, especially her vagina, is man's property, and, like any other property, can be stolen by those to whom it does not belong

(3) the view that "good" women must defend that property at almost any cost

(4) the idea that normal males will not need to resort to force in order to acquire the sexual property represented by women

MYTHS ABOUT RAPE

Myths have a manifest purpose of legitimating aberrant behavior. This is especially true where rape is concerned. Mayerson and Taylor (1987) state that women as well as men believe in many rape myths and are aroused by rape depictions. Men, for example, may believe that a woman will respond positively to sexual force even if she initially refuses sexual advances. There are many such myths that center on the commission of rape, be it date rape, power or anger rape, or rape within marriage.

One myth is that *rape is a crime caused by uncontrollable sex drive*. Men who are in prison for serial rape and serial murder involving sexual abuse often claim that they felt such a compulsion for sex that they could not help themselves. However, this argument does not appear to be valid; virtually all such men are either married or otherwise have available sex partners when they commit their crimes (Amir, 1971; Groth, 1979; Groth & Burgess, 1977; MacDonald, 1971).

A second myth is that *women can resist rape if they want to*. This suggests that any woman can successfully fight off a man if she does not want to be raped (sometimes the argument is stated as "You can't thread a moving needle"). This is obviously untrue. First of all, men have been raised differently from women. Men have been trained to be physical and, for the most part, men are stronger and faster than women. By the same token, women traditionally have been trained to be passive, weaker, and receptive to men. Such socialization no doubt enhances the possibility of a "successful" rape. In addition, it is the rapist who chooses the place and the time for the rape to occur—the woman has little to do with the situation other than being in the wrong place at the wrong time.

Rapes are committed by strangers is yet another widely believed myth. Walker (1988, p. 27) states that the importance of prior relationships is most dramatically evident in the case of rape. According to Turner (1988), about half of all sexual assaults on adult women are committed by men who know their victims; Walker (1988) suggests that the proportion may be as high as 80%. Date rape, acquaintance rape, and marital rape (which will be covered later in this chapter) are all examples of rape where the rapist is known to the victim. In some states—Kentucky, for example—there is no law that makes it a crime for a husband to rape his wife.

A fourth myth is that *many women falsely cry rape*. It is no doubt true that some women report rape when it has not occurred (for revenge or for some other reason), but it would be a gross mistake to assume that the majority of rape cases reported to the police are false. Historically, it has been more likely for women *not* to report rape that *has* occurred. As Crooks and Baur (1983, p. 615) point out, in the past, women who failed to report rape may have had good reason, as they themselves often faced severe persecution when they made such charges. If some women had not had the courage to face that persecution, however, few rape cases today could be prosecuted successfully.

All women want to be raped is a myth that has been "romanticized" in the media. The paperback "romance" story often starts with the female resisting the advances and even the sexual attack of the rapist only to "melt into passionate acceptance" (Crooks & Baur, 1983). It is true that some women do have rape fantasies, but these fantasies typically do not center on the use of force or pain but on a feeling of "being swept off one's feet" by a tall, dark, and handsome stranger into a sexual liaison that one would not ordinarily entertain.

It can't happen to me is a delusional belief that many women hold. Accepting the myth that rape victims are always young and attractive, many believe that they are unlikely to be victims because they are too old, too thin, too heavy, or otherwise not "desirable." It must be remembered that rape is a crime of violence and not of sex. Sexual attractiveness is not a selective trait used by rapists when they are stalking their victims.

REASONS FOR NOT REPORTING RAPE

Myths abound about rape for other reasons, one of which is the lack of knowledge about such behavior. Rape is one of the most underreported crimes committed. The crime is one of degradation as well as violence, and fear of reprisal and embarrassment contributes to the victim's hesitation to report it. Those who do report it must confront the trauma of the encounter with the police, the investigation of the crime, and the ordeal of the trial.

It is probably true that only 10% of all rapes are reported (Nelton, 1987); we know little about the circumstances of the other 90%. Hagan (1990, p. 236) reports that women are reluctant to report rape for the following reasons:

(1) the stigma attached to rape victims

(2) the sexist treatment given to many women, who are in effect mentally raped a second time by the criminal justice system

(3) legal procedures that in the past have permitted courtroom prosecutors to probe the victim's sexual past, which can be both humiliating and embarrassing

(4) the fact that the burden of proof often has been shifted to the victim, who must prove that the attack was forced and against her will and that she resisted the attack

The U.S. Department of Justice (1987, p. 8) has stated that women do not report rapes because they feel the incidents are too personal or that the police will be insensitive.

Men too are raped, although male rape is a less established custom in our culture than is female rape. It is probable that, like female rape cases, many male rape cases go unreported. It appears that the male ego and fear of loss of reputation keep many men from admitting to having been raped (Kaufman, 1980).

The underreporting of rape cases can lead to assumptions regarding rape that are diametrically opposed to the knowledge that actually exists. It may also be true that since only a small percentage of all rapes are reported, and the knowledge we have regarding rape, rapists, and rape victims is gleaned from crisis centers and the police, there is a huge sampling problem involved in making statements regarding rape using this data base (Orlando & Koss, 1983).

RAPE AND THE LAW

Since ancient times, the rape victim has been viewed as a "fallen woman"—one who deserved, invited, or contributed to the sexual assault upon her. Rape prosecution in the United States is very difficult, to say the least. Often the woman herself is once again "assaulted" by the police and the court system. Despite the rape shield law, which prevents the defense from bringing up the victim's sexual history in court, the judge and jury often hear intimate personal details of her past life. Unfortunately, this can have an effect on some jury members' minds during their deliberations.

The court has to deal with the legal issues of corroboration and consent in rape prosecution. The prosecution must prove that a rape did indeed occur—that there was sexual penetration, that some type of force was used, and that consent was absent. Some states still require the testimony of an eyewitness, other than the victim, for conviction. The jury must be convinced that sexual penetration took place, which demands some type of medical testimony. Detailed medical information is shared with the court regarding the physical condition of the victim when she was examined, the condition of her clothing and other personal effects, the presence of semen and/or blood, and other items that must be preserved in some type of chain of evidence.

As times have changed, so have laws regarding rape. Some states have moved away from the traditional point of view that sexual penetration is necessary for rape to occur. Oral sex is included in this new definition, as is

TABLE 7.1. Types of Rape and Legal Defenses

Category	Legal Defenses
Forcible rape by a stranger	The accused is a victim of mistaken identification by the victim.
Forcible rape by a friend	The victim is now changing her story; she was willing to have sex.
Nonforcible rape with underaged person	The accused mistakenly thought that the victim was of age, or sex did not occur.
Nonforcible rape with one unable to give consent	The accused did not know of the victim's disability, or the act did not occur.
Nonforcible rape with unconscious victim	The victim was conscious and consented, or the act did not occur.
Sex with deception	No deception was involved, or no sex occurred.
Sex through threats	No threat was made or no sex occurred.

SOURCE: Adapted from Gardner (1989).

object penetration; anal rape is also now considered. Resistance now does not have to be proven. Some states are now realizing that men too are raped and women are also rapists, and laws use gender-neutral terms for both the offender and the victim. The definition of force now includes threats of violence and the use of physical force to restrain or control a victim. If little or no actual force was used in the rape, the state must demonstrate that the woman's resistance was overcome by the threat of force (Gardner, 1989, p. 457). (See Table 7.1 for a list of types of rapes and the legal defenses that are often associated with them.)

It appears now that the essential elements of the crime of forcible rape include the following (Gardner, 1989, p. 456):

(1) proof that a sex act has occurred (as defined by the statute)

(2) proof that force (actual or threatened) was used to perform the sex act

(3) proof that the sex act occurred "without the consent" and "against the will" of the victim (these terms being synonymous in the law of rape)

Of course, there are good reasons for care to be taken in the prosecution of accused rapists. An example of what can happen is the case of Gary Dotson, who was sent to prison for the rape of Cathleen Webb. The case received national attention when Webb confessed that she had lied to the court and had accused Dotson falsely, resulting in his incarceration. He was released by the governor of Illinois. It appears that the courts and jurors are especially careful in rape trials to avoid convicting anyone who is truly innocent.

CHARACTERISTICS OF RAPISTS

Rapists are typically young. Some 80% are under the age of 30, and 75% are under the age of 25 (Queen's Bench Foundation, 1976). They are most often from the lower socioeconomic class, are often minority group members, and typically choose victims of their own race (Hagan, 1990). The psychosexual backgrounds of rapists often include families with histories of conflict and special problems in relating to women. Rapists tend to see men as being the takers in sex and women as the givers (Turner, 1988, p. 108; Walker, 1988, p. 27). As discussed above, most rapes are committed by men who know their victims.

Most rapists are unarmed; in one of every four cases where the rapist is armed, the weapon is a knife. Most plan their attacks, although Haas and Haas (1990) state that in their sample, half of the rapists decided to rape on the spur of the moment. Rapists usually have a history of violence; one in three has a prior record of violent crime, and 25% have previously been before the court for rape.

Hazelwood and Warren (1989), who interviewed 41 rapists in prison, found that the serial rapist more often than not comes from an average or advantaged home and as an adult is a well-groomed, intelligent, employed individual who is living with others in a family context. The greatest pathology is reflected in the rapists' developmental histories. Few of the men described close relationships with either of their parents, and 76% reported either observing sexual acts or being sexually abused as children or adolescents. As children, 15% of the rapists reported residing in orphanages, 41% in detention homes, 8% in foster homes, 26% in mental health facilities, and 4% in boarding homes or military schools. The majority of these rapists' victims were strangers who, in almost half of the cases, were assaulted in their homes. As far as victim selection was concerned, "availability" was an important factor.

Vinogradov, Dishotsky, Doty, and Tinklenberg (1988) studied adolescent rapists and found that the typical adolescent rape takes place on a weekend night around the end of summer vacation. This rape usually occurs in the victim's home or in an automobile. During the adolescent rape, it is common to have multiple rapists (gang rape). This rapist is typically a young male who is from the lower social class and who has a history of prior arrests. This rapist may also carry some type of weapon. The victim is usually a female who is a stranger to the rapist, and the rapist has no sexual interest in the victim. Many rapists, both adolescents and others, are under the influence of alcohol or drugs when they rape (Rodenas, Osuna, & Luna, 1989).

PSYCHOLOGY OF RAPE

If rape is a crime of violence and sex is the weapon used, certain psychological elements are present, elements that are analogous to those found in other types of personal violent crimes. In addition to these, there appear to be other important elements: power, anger, and sexuality (Groth, Burgess, & Holstrom 1977).

There is no simple explanation for the etiology of a rapist. Moreover, not all rapists are alike. Motives, expectations, gains, and anticipations all vary from one rapist to another. But there are some studies that shed some light on the personality of the rapist. The relationship between the mother and the rapist has been a major focus of research. The father, on the other hand, appears to be less significant. The mother is typically described as being rejecting of the rapist as a child, domineering, punitive, overprotective, and seductive. The father is described as uninvolved, aloof, distant, absent, or passive, but occasionally punitive and cruel. Parental cruelty, inconsistency of discipline, envy, and sexual frustration also play a role in the development of a rapist (Holmes, 1983; Rada, 1978).

Parental seduction, usually involving the mother, occurs continuously, from covert seduction to actual sexual involvement. There may be a history of early, prolonged bed sharing with a sibling or a parent, which may sensitize the child's imagination unduly to sexual stimulation. In some cases, sharing of the bed with the mother is prolonged into puberty.

Many rapists also have histories of severe physical punishment by their dominating, sadistic, and castrating mothers. The father, because of his personality, may not lend support to the child when it is really needed. If the mother is cruel, dominating, and so on, the rapist's future hostility may be directed toward women in general because of the pain he suffered from a woman (Holmes, 1989, p. 102).

Exhibit 7.2

Rapists Are Often . . .

very attractive men.

in their late teens through mid-30s.

married or with a sexual partner.

fathers of small children still at home.

of average or above-average intelligence.

in jobs that require travel.

respected in their neighborhoods.

insecure; their childhoods are often marked by cruelty.

SOURCE: Rape Relief Center, Louisville, Kentucky (1990).

The research on rape shows generally that the rapist is not brain damaged or possessed of a marked mental pathology (Hagan, 1990, p. 204). Conversely, there is some evidence that shows that about 10% of rapists are psychotic at the time of the rape, and an additional 60% are sociopaths (Groth, 1979, pp. 106-109).

TYPES OF RAPISTS

There appear to be at least three types of rapists. Research by Knight and Prentky (1987) illustrates very well the types based on anger and power. (For a detailed examination of rape, see Holmes, 1989.)

The *power rapist* suffers from great personal insecurity. He has an overwhelming fear of impotence and doubts about his own masculinity. He often compensates for these feelings of inadequacy by controlling others. This rapist believes that women like to be raped and often dates women prior to raping them. Such a rapist may also ask a woman for a date after he has raped her. In one case, a rapist asked his victim after he raped her if she had enjoyed it. In her own way of handling the situation, she said that he was kind and gentle in raping her, more gentle than her husband. He then suggested that he come back the next day at 9:00 in the morning, and she agreed. She called the police after he left, and they were awaiting him when he returned the next

Exhibit 7.3

He did not kill me, but
he did kill the person I was.

SOURCE: A rape victim (1990).

morning. This rapist was "appalled" when the police arrested him as he climbed through the bedroom window.

The *anger rapist* believes that he must retaliate for an imagined wrong or loss. This type of rapist usually feels some type of conflict within his personality that impels him from a psychological state of equilibrium into a fall of assault toward a victim. These assaults are often unplanned, explosive attacks directed toward randomly selected victims. Sex is the weapon used, and the rapist will vent his rage and anger by beating and degrading his victim. He may force her into aberrant sexual acts, and may use vulgar language as a means of both intimidation and degradation. Often this rapist has a history of aggressive and violent crimes.

The *sadistic rapist* seeks revenge and punishment from another person by the use of violence and cruelty. The victim is typically only a symbol of the source of his anger. This sex criminal is very deliberate in his rapes and plans each one very carefully. Ted Bundy, in addition to being a serial killer, must be viewed as a serial sadistic rapist. As he related to me during a session on death row, "A large number of serial killings are an attempt to silence the victims, an extreme but simple form of elimination" (author's files).

The sadistic rapist often is very ritualistic in his attacks on women. The victims themselves are often traumatized, suffer extreme physical injuries, and, in many cases, are murdered.

The *gang rapist* rapes in the company of his peers. Reducing the victim to the low status of an object, the gang rapist seeks confirmation of his own masculinity and expresses power and authority over another person, validating his superior position. The ages of gang rapists vary. They can be as young as 10 years old, but the upper age cohort appears to be in the mid-30s. In true gang behavior, the first person to rape the helpless victim is typically the leader of the gang. It is also interesting that the age of the victim usually reflects the age of the gang members.

The *date rapist* or *acquaintance rapist* is someone who is known to the victim and who forces unwanted sexual advances on her. Date rape is a phenomenon that surpasses physical abuse (Stets & Pirog-Good, 1989).

It is becoming a recognized problem on many college campuses, although of course it is not confined to students. Even among high school students, it is estimated that over 30% of female students are sexually or physically abused in dating relationships (McShane, 1988). Some people feel that since the rapist and the victim know each other, date rape is not as serious as stranger rape. This should not be an issue, of course. The criminal justice system should not view this sexual assault as any different from any other in its seriousness (Giacopassi, 1987).

It appears that the rate of date rape has increased dramatically since the 1950s. This trend in sexual violence in dating may be the result of several factors: increased sexual freedom of young females in social and sexual relationships with male counterparts, the unrestrained portrayal of human sexuality in the mass media, and the widespread use of alcohol and drugs (Levine & Kanin, 1987).

It is likely that the rate of reporting of date rape is no higher than that for stranger-perpetrated rape. Parrot (1989), for example, states that most date-rape victims have low self-esteem and believe that the violent acts that have taken place were beyond their control; most have also experienced past victimizations. She adds that it is difficult to identify these victims because many are reluctant to report the rapes; many may not even recognize their rapes as sexual assaults. Victims may also know that date rape trials seldom end in conviction, and thus may be reluctant to report.

CONCLUSION

It is imperative that a concentrated effort be directed toward encouraging the reporting of all cases of the violent crime of rape. This is the ideal, but unfortunately there is little chance that this will come about in the near future, for the reasons discussed in this chapter. Victims must be comfortable in dealing with the criminal justice system, and must be able to trust that the system will not victimize them again. Society must recognize, and rape victims must be assured, that women are not to blame when they are raped. No one asks or deserves to be raped.

Further, vigorous and effective treatment programs for rapists should be increased to combat the very real danger these offenders present to our society. Until this is done, the vicious crime of rape will continue to claim victims.

8

Pornography: Adult and Child

There are few more difficult moral social issues confronting Americans than the debate concerning pornography and obscenity. There are many arguments regarding the effects, both positive and negative, of exposure to erotica. National organizations such as Citizens for Decency Through the Law (CDTL) have been established to lobby for legislation to combat the perceived dangers of pornography and obscenity in the courts of this country.

What is lacking in this debate is any thorough empirical examination of pornography and obscenity and their effects. It is often suggested that exposure to pornography leads those exposed to serious sex crimes. However, data presented in this chapter suggest that such exposure does not necessarily lead to the commission of sex crimes by someone who is otherwise a social human being. The content of the sexual messages, the amount and character of personal violence, the debasement of women, and so on may have more to do with the predelictions of the viewer than with the pornography itself.

This chapter examines two types of pornography: adult pornography and child pornography. Relevant research is discussed, as well as the effects of this research on policy issues and human behavior.

PORNOGRAPHY AND OBSCENITY

In any examination of pornography there emerges immediately the issue of defining pornography and obscenity. This should be the first thing addressed by any decisive examination. The word *pornography* literally means "the writings of harlots." In the early history of humankind, paintings that depicted men and women in sexual scenes were found on the walls of caves. In ancient Mesopotamia, for example, Baal and Ishtar, Marduk, humans, animals, and others were depicted in sexual scenes on dinner plates, washbasins, water holders, and other household goods. Today, a debate exists concerning whether or not this type of material can be classified as pornography.

There is also argument over what constitutes obscenity. What is obscene and what is not? This is a question that is very difficult to address and debate adequately (Abraham, Hill, Orlofsky, Sass, & Sobel, 1980). Pornography is not difficult to define. Pornography is *not* a subjective evaluation from the point of view of the customer who buys *Playboy* magazine. Pornography is material produced for the manifest purpose of arousing erotic feelings. The primary motive for producing a painting, a book, a statue, a movie, or a music album may be to make money, but if a secondary reason is to arouse erotic feelings within the buyer or the viewer, it is pornography. Works of art that include nudity, such as Michelangelo's statue of David or the Venus de Milo, are never defined by serious critics as pornography. Medical textbooks that show sexual organs and parts of the body that normally are sexual in nature are seldom viewed as pornographic. But when one views the centerfold of a *Playboy* magazine, there is little doubt about the motivation of the model, the photographer, or the publisher. The depiction of Miss July is intended for arousal of the viewer as well as to make money. The deliberate exposure of certain body parts is intended to arouse sexual feelings and also obviously to make money.

The definition of obscenity is rather more subjective. Obscenity can be defined as anything that is disgusting to the senses. There are issues and behaviors that are obscene but not pornographic—war, for example. For many, war is obscene under any circumstances. The conflict in Vietnam was judged to be obscene by untold thousands of people in the United States. Child sexual and physical abuse is obscene. Poverty, spouse abuse, and many other social problems that have nothing to do with sexual arousal are judged by many to be obscene.

Obscenity's subjective dimension causes a great deal of consternation among groups lobbying for action against pornography. A standard has been developed to measure what qualifies as pornography. But obscenity is an entirely different story.

STANDARDS OF OBSCENITY

There have been numerous attempts to regulate obscenity throughout the United States. Some groups, such as Citizens for Decency Through the Law, are involved in pushing for legislation against pornography. CDTL was founded by Charles Keating, who is currently being sued by the state of California for alleged fraud in the sale of $250 million in now worthless junk bonds, particularly victimizing the elderly (*USA Today*, June 28, 1990, p. B1). Many would judge the bilking of the elderly, many on fixed incomes, as obscene.

Obscenity is not protected by the First Amendment and may be forbidden and regulated by government (Gardner, 1989, p. 244). The case of *Miller v. California* (413 U.S. 15, 93 S.Ct. 2607, 1973) was such an attempt to settle once and for all the debate over what is obscene. There are three standards used to determine what is pornographic and obscene:

(1) whether "the average person applying contemporary community standards" would find that the work, taken as a whole, appeals to prurient interest (i.e., appeals to sexual interest, causing a person to become sexually aroused)

(2) whether the work or communication depicts or describes, in a patently offensive way, sexual conduct specifically defined by the applicable state law

(3) whether the work of communication, taken as a whole, lacks serious literary, artistic, political, or scientific value

CUSTOMERS FOR PORNOGRAPHY

It appears that most consumers of pornography are young, married males. The majority are college-educated, white-collar workers. Approximately 25% of all consumers of pornography have been exposed to some sadomasochistic material.

John B, an incarcerated pedophile who used to work as a counter salesperson at an adult porn bookstore, told me in an interview that his store kept the child pornography under the counter and would sell the material only to customers who had become fairly well known. He stated that there were no distinguishing factors he could ascertain when selling the kiddie porn. The

TABLE 8.1. Numbers and Pornography

Number of sexually explicit videotapes rented each year: 348 million

Annual cost of rentals of sexually explicit videotapes: $768 million

Breakdown of rentals: rentals by men, 53%; rentals by women, 18%;
  rentals by couples, 29%

Number of adult videotapes released in 1983, 400; in 1985, 1,600;
  in 1989, 1,300

SOURCE: *Playboy* (July 1990).

customers were mostly white businessmen who came into the shop during their lunch hours.

Most of the consumers of adult pornography do have sex partners, and use the pornography to enhance their own sex lives with those partners. Younger consumers and many others use pornography for masturbatory functions (Nawy, 1973; Wilson & Abelson, 1973). (See Table 8.1 for some figures on pornographic videotape customers.)

PORNOGRAPHY, RESEARCH, AND THE SEX CRIMINAL

The central issue here is the relationship between sex crimes and exposure to erotica. Various studies have examined this relationship. In 1970, the President's Commission on Obscenity and Pornography failed to reach a firm conclusion regarding exposure to pornography and sex offenses. Discounting the possible (some might say probable) relationship between child pornography and sex crimes against children, principally because of the lack of child pornography materials and observations that existed in U.S. society 20 years ago, the statements this commission made regarding pornography were directed toward adult pornography. The majority statement made by the commission members was that adult erotic materials should be available for all those persons over the age of 18 who desire to look at said materials. Since there was no finding of a causal relationship between exposure to erotic materials and sex crimes, the commission believed that banning such materials would not serve a positive societal function.

Of course, not all members of the group believed in this position. Charles Keating, then a congressman from Ohio, stated that pornography should be banned for all persons regardless of age. His classic statement, "Those who wallow in filth will get dirty," has been quoted and misquoted many times since he uttered it almost 20 years ago.

Another minority statement was issued by Larsen and Wolfgang, who took the position that pornography should be made available to anyone, regardless of age. Their position was that, since there were no reliable data showing a direct causal relationship between such exposure and the development of a sex offender, and since there was no way to regulate the sale and distribution of such material, it would be simpler and better not to attempt to limit its sale.

Kant and Goldstein (1973) studied three groups of men: "normals" (occasional viewers of pornographic material), "users" (regular purchasers and viewers of pornography), and "sex offenders" (incarcerated rapists, child molesters of young boys, and child molesters of young girls who were free the year prior to the study). Two particularly important questions were asked of all the groups. One question was, "As an adolescent, how much pornography did you see?" Carefully measuring quantity, Kant and Goldstein found that sex offenders all reported less exposure to pornographic material than did the other two groups. A second question addressed the men's exposure to pornography "last year." The time frame was important because the sex offenders had all been free the previous year. Again, the sex offenders reported seeing less pornography than the other two groups. One finding of this study is that exposure to pornography may play a positive role in the maturational process of non-sex offenders. The most important finding is that sex criminals, not only as adolescents but also as adults, see less pornography than do normals or users.

PORNOGRAPHY AND VIOLENCE

Regardless of these findings, there are many who believe that exposure to pornographic materials necessarily leads a person to commit sex crimes against women. S. McCarthy (1982) believes that the findings of the President's Commission noted above are no longer valid since the character of pornography has changed a great deal since the early 1970s. One important difference may be the amount of violence present in contemporary pornography.

Fishbach and Malamuth (1978) suggest a link between exposure to violent pornography and sex crimes against women. Their position has been validated by others (Goode, 1984; Malamuth & Donnerstein, 1982). In a study of 54 college-aged males, Heilbrun and Seif (1988) found that men who viewed violent erotic pictures of women in physical distress in bondage found it to be more sexually stimulating than a female model displayed in a more positive setting. Linz (1989) found that long-term exposure to violent pornography (slasher films) resulted in consistently less sensitivity toward rape victims among a male sample.

Consider the following comments made by a serial killer currently in prison in California during my interview with him:

> The history of my own rise to serial murder cannot be told or understood without first mentioning the person and the deeds of someone I met a very long time ago. For it can be said of this person—this man, to be exact—that he was the one who planted within me the seeds of what would later bloom into full-scale sexual violence. This is not to say that he was directly responsible for my becoming a serial killer, as there were many other factors that would also come into play, and no single thing "made" me into a man of violence. Nevertheless, it remains true that this man would play a very large role in starting me on the long and twisted course that would ultimately lead to murder.
>
> From what I can recall of him, he was very tall and exceptionally thin, a stooped-over figure who was always given to wearing a heavy black coat that dragged along the floor as he walked. He made his home in a large, somber, and foreboding castle that had many cheerless rooms within its thick, stone walls. And, in keeping with the gloomy character of his ancient castle residence, he himself was a sullen and very sinister-looking man. Indeed, he had a face that could easily pass for a clean but living skull, were it not for the barest layer of flesh and skin that stretched tightly over his bony features.
>
> The first time I ever met this man, he was shuffling into one of the torch-lit chambers beneath his castle, a menacing expression on his ugly face as he made his way toward a large, odd-shaped table in the middle of the room. On the top of the wooden table there was a frightened young actress whom he had kidnapped earlier in the same day. He had already stripped away all of her clothing, so the woman lay nude and sprawled on her back, her limbs strapped down in a helpless, spread-eagled position. When the man reached the table, I recall that he lowered his hand and started caressing the young woman's face, telling her that she had nothing to worry about, in spite of her very terrifying predicament. After all, she was a "guest" in his house, he said to her, and thus she would receive only "the very best of treatment" while she remained under his care.
>
> After feeding her this line of phony reassurance, however, the man started torturing the young actress by wrapping his fingers around one of her breasts

and slowly tightening his grip. As he gradually increased the pressure of his squeezing fingers, he scanned up and down the length of the woman's body, his eyes waiting eagerly to see the first signs of struggle that she would make against the pain he was causing her. And, when she finally jerked against the bonds encircling her ankles and wrists, the man responded to this movement by stepping on a lever that activated a small motor underneath the table. To the woman's horror, a pair of slats beneath her lower limbs started spreading open automatically, forcing her legs to stretch even wider and more painfully apart. And, as the muscles in her legs began to strain and knot up from this new ordeal, the man continued closing his bony fingers, digging them deeper and more cruelly into her naked breasts.

The young actress screamed. Yet even as the chamber reverberated with the sound of her piercing shrieks, the man was not the least bit moved by his captive's terror or her cries of pain. Indeed, each time the woman was overcome by pain to the point where she slipped away into unconsciousness, the man simply revived her and started up the torture yet again. He tortured her until she could scream no more—until her mind, like her body, was a broken shell—and then he triumphantly proceeded to rape her where she lay. After assaulting her, he killed her on the spot. Finally, then, being satisfied with the job that he had done, the man cleared the table of his victim's corpse and began thinking ahead to the next young woman who would lay there strapped down on its surface.

The man and the deeds I've just described are actually the ghosts of a paperback novel that came into my hands a little over 25 years ago. Quite clearly, as should be gathered from the brief yet highly sanitized dungeon scene that I've recounted here, the story of this fictional castle-dweller was both sadistic and obscene. Indeed, from its opening page to its closing chapter, this book seemed to have no other purpose than to depict sexual violence in the most painstaking detail and as the kind of treatment that women generally deserved. In short, this paperback novel was violent pornography at its worst—a perverse and graphically written tribute to the sexual brutalization of female human beings.

This recounting shows that this serial murderer's exposure to violent pornography at the age of 9 left a lasting impression upon his psyche. This paperback novel provided a script that he would use over and over again in his sadistic torture and murder of numerous young women. It did not cause him to be a serial killer, but it did provide him with some rationalizations and methods of murder. Marshall (1988) found that rapists reported frequent use of pornography prior to committing the act of rape. It provides them a script for action.

Padgett and Brislin-Slutz (1989) report that patrons of adult theaters, who view more pornography than college students who were also studied, have more favorable attitudes toward women, and attitudes toward women are not influenced by type of exposure. In addition, pornography may become for some a source of sex education. This is supported by research conducted by Tjaden (1988), who found significant differences between young men's and young women's uses of pornography as a sex education tool.

The Attorney General's Office (1986) report on pornography concludes that some forms of pornography cause sex crimes. This report has been severely criticized for various methodological reasons; according to critics, the authors fail to observe research guidelines and make gross assumptions that are not supported by the data collected (Lynn, 1986; Nobile & Nadler, 1986; Scott, 1988).

The central issue in the relationship between sex crimes and exposure to pornography is the long-term effect that this exposure may have on a person. Long-term effects have yet to be found in the research done by serious social and behavioral scientists. It may be that "exposure to violent pornography does not necessarily cause such callous attitudes, but may simply reinforce and strengthen attitudes that people already hold" (Conklin, 1989, p. 274). Exposure to sexually explicit materials does not in itself foster negative attitudes or behavior in men's relationships with women. But there is some evidence that repeated exposure to pornography coupled with violence may decrease inhibitions for some and lead to some victimization (Donnerstein, Linz, & Penrod, 1987).

CHILD PORNOGRAPHY

Perhaps nothing causes as much outrage toward obscenity as child pornography. Commonly called "kiddie porn," this type of pornography has been universally legislated against in the United States. However, most of the child pornography that is confiscated by law enforcement officials in the United States has been imported from foreign countries.

Child Pornography and the Law

Prior to 1977, there were few laws on either the state or the federal level that regulated the production, distribution, or sale of child pornography. Today, however, almost every state and the federal government have laws that prescribe penalties against those who exploit children sexually. The

Protection of Children Against Sexual Exploitation Act, Public Law 95-225, extended the federal government's role to include prosecution of those involved in child pornography. This law has also made it illegal to transport children across state lines for immoral purposes.

A total of 48 states have passed legislation concerning child pornography. More than a few states have merely amended their adult pornography laws to include acts that involve children. Other states, however, have devised new laws that deal specifically with children. Under these laws, penalties are ascribed to those who use children in a sexual performance, promote a sexual performance by a minor, or distribute and sell materials that depict children in sexual scenes. The fundamental question of defining pornography is not addressed and is only vaguely alluded to by the inclusion of a broad, three-pronged requirement for obscenity and an accompanying definition of "sexual performance" (Pope, 1978).

Types of Child Pornography

Many publications exist that cater to adults who are interested in seeing children posed in sexual situations. One study estimates there are as many as 264 different magazines produced and sold in adult bookstores in the United States that deal with sexual acts between children or between children and adults (Densen-Gerber & Hutchison, 1978). Interestingly enough, in my dealings with pedophiles I have never been involved with any who did not have some type of kiddie porn in their possession. Some of this pornography was "home-made" (as in the case of the pedophile who wrote the story "The Earthquake," which was related in Chapter 1), and some was of the commercial variety.

There are several types of commercial kiddie porn. First of all, there are magazines that are not unlike *Playboy* or *Penthouse*. These magazines contain pictorial essays of young boys or girls in sexually suggestive poses as well as letters from adults who desire to have sex with children or who describe their sexual activities with children. These magazines typically cater to pedophiles who are interested in having sex with either young males or young females. It is unusual, for example, for a kiddie porn magazine to contains photos and stories about both sexes.

Publications such as *Lollitots* and *Lolita* are aimed at pedophiles interested only in young girls. These magazines contain pictures of young females, often engaged in poses that are obviously designed to arouse erotic feelings. There are also editorials that reflect a philosophy that the real dangers to our society are the widely held negative attitudes regarding child nudity and sex with children. *Piccolo, Bare Boys,* and *Tommy* are examples of kiddie porn that caters to the homosexual pedophile. The contents of these magazines are similar to those of the publications that feature young girls.

Another type of kiddie porn takes the character of paperback novels. In these books, a child typically becomes the object of the sexual aggression of the viewer. These paperback novels often contain graphic violence directed against a child, a powerful adult figure who victimizes a child, and a final scene where the victimization becomes cyclical.

Photographs purchased through the mail and ads exchanged through computer bulletin boards are other methods of kiddie porn exchange. Personal computers with telephone modems have opened the door for many pedophiles to contact other pedophiles for the purpose of swapping child pornography as well as children themselves.

Relational pornography also takes various forms. Poems, stories written by those interested in sex with children, and newspaper advertisements that feature children in swim wear or underwear all become items of sexual arousal for some pedophiles. These ads in themselves are not pornographic in nature—they are intended only as sales promotions. However, when they interact with the fantasy of the pedophile, they can become a form of kiddie porn.

Who Sees Kiddie Porn

There are several audiences for child pornography. Obviously, pedophiles compose the largest number of people who view kiddie porn. Just as "normal" adults view pornography for various reasons, including sexual arousal, so do pedophiles. The curious form another group of persons who view kiddie porn. Many wish to see such pornography because they have not seen it before; they are simply curious about the content. For most of these viewers, this is a one-time occasion.

Yet another group is composed of those persons who are involved in the manufacture of child pornography. A great deal of child pornography comes from Scandinavian countries; it is also produced in Mexico, Spain, the United States, and other countries. The persons involved in the production of such materials must view their own products as well as those of others, to see what topics are "hot" in kiddie porn.

Lured into prostitution and then pornography, pimps are often involved. With promises of friendship, money, or drugs, pimps locate clients for kiddie porn. McKinnon (1979) states that child porn materials are marketed through a subculture of black-market contacts who make them available to ready customers.

There are legitimate reasons to view child pornography. Law enforcement and other social, political, or educational groups must sometimes view this material to gauge the content and to judge its legal status, or to formulate some type of psychological profile of the person who possesses such materials. I have consulted with several police departments on the content of child pornography to give the police an idea as to the personality of the owner.

How Are Children Involved in Pornography?

It appears that children who become involved in kiddie porn come from sources both wide and diverse (Holmes, 1984; Schultz, 1980). First, there are "sporting clubs" (Bahlmann & Thomas, 1979; Holmes, 1983) composed of parents who arrange for their children to appear in sexually oriented photographs. There are parents who swap photographs, videos, and films of their children with other parents and commercial enterprises for fun and profit.

Burdiit (1978) states that often children who are involved in pornography are intimidated by adults who hold power over them. Schultz (1980) reports a case of one couple who took in children off the streets, who would then have to pay their "rent" by performing in kiddie porn productions. In another case, a couple with a 6-month-old child was arrested by police when it became known that they were involving their infant in childhood prostitution with men. In addition to the prostitution case, the police discovered the father was filming the sex between the child and the adults and selling the videos as child pornography. The couple were granted probation by the court, and the child was released to their custody.

In Illinois, a summer camp was found to be a front for enticing children into child porn. Confidential film-developing services are yet another source. But despite the widespread belief that organized crime is involved in the child pornography industry, this does not appear to be the case (Illinois Legislative Investigative Committee, 1980).

Who Are the Children in Child Pornography?

There is a lack of empirical research into determining the extent and the characteristics of the children who are involved in child pornography. C. Baker (1978) states that there are over 30,000 children annually involved in the kiddie porn industry; more than 3,000 under the age of 14 are in Los Angeles alone.

Some characteristics appear to be common among children involved in child pornography:

(1) involvement in childhood prostitution

(2) runaway

(3) broken home

(4) between the ages of 8 and 17

(5) underachiever in school or home

(6) no strong moral or religious affiliation

(7) poor social development

(8) parents physically or psychologically absent

In an unpublished study I conducted for the Exploited and Missing Child Unit in Louisville, Kentucky, I interviewed 34 juveniles who admitted being involved in child pornography. Their social core variables showed interesting similarities. For example, children involved in the kiddie porn industry are frequently runaways. Some children flee their homes because of abuse, rigid discipline, or a variety of other reasons, such as pregnancy or emotional problems. Family disorganization and discord are associated with juvenile participation in kiddie porn. The youths reported that few of their parents were married (14.6%), and only one in five admitted to having a close relationship with his or her parents. Only 20% reported close relationships with their brothers and sisters. The responses of this sample indicate a malaise in relationships within the family. Although the data obtained in this study suggest a high rate of divorce within such families, marital status may not be as important as the amount of conflict present in the family. Divorce, as a process, may be a problem-solving technique and may create a situation that is healthier than the one that might exist if the conflicting parents remain together.

Without exception, the children admitted to the use of alcohol and drugs, especially marijuana and amphetamines. In more than four of five cases, the children said they had run away from home—another indication of family discord. Perhaps because of the problems in the home—with discord, aggression, hostility, and anomie—the runaway behavior may be viewed as another problem-solving technique. But in most cases this behavior results only in the child's moving from one bad situation to another. Involvement in child pornography may be a matter of survival for many children, as is involvement in prostitution for many young persons.

The general findings of this study indicate a psychological profile of a child who comes from a home where loving and caring are not expressed, where discord is common, and where there is frequent abuse and drug abuse. This is the making of a child involved in the kiddie porn industry.

CONCLUSION

The issue of pornography remains a serious one. Much energy is expended on developing social policies and programs to deal with the effects of pornographic material. Needed legislation should be enacted regarding the involvement of children in pornography. Since children are vulnerable and helpless, special attention needs to be paid to finding ways to protect them. Vigorous social action needs to be directed at those adults who victimize children and involve them in any form of child pornography.

In the case of adult pornography, a different approach may be warranted. Many Americans are not in favor of government censoring of reading and viewing materials for any reason. They feel they have the right to view and to read anything they desire, and are vehemently opposed to any infringement on that right. In any case, it is clear that additional research needs to be done regarding the effects of adult pornography on sexual behavior.

9

Victims of Sexual Assault

Most Americans believe they will never be victims of violent sex crimes. This thought itself serves as psychological insulation from disturbing thoughts of being victimized by rapists, lust murderers, or picquerists. Some statistics are available on the likelihood of becoming a victim. A profile of the typical crime victim (without specifying type of crime) shows that the individual is a young Black male who is single, poor, and unemployed.

Untold numbers of people are victims of some kinds of sex crimes and are not aware of it at the time. In my classes at the University of Louisville, I ask my students if they have even been in a crowded place and felt a hand on their bodies where that hand should not be. The majority of the students, both males and females, respond in a positive fashion. They have been victims of frotteurs. Additionally, many young women will admit that they have been victims of flashers. These victims typically respond in a light tone, usually saying that the man simply turned and ran or drove away.

Some have been victimized in more unique ways. For example, one of my students, a young woman, stated that a man called her on the phone and claimed that he was a physician. He offered her a free medical examination if she would cooperate with his interview. He contended that he had patented a medical device that could telephonically detect lumps in the woman's breasts if she would only hold the receiver against each breast as he adjusted the dials. The young woman did as she was told. As the "examination" proceeded, he reported that the medical mechanism was getting a reading, but she would have to move the phone speaker in a more circular motion around her breasts. Finally becoming suspicious, she hung up the phone. Nothing extreme in nature happened to this young woman; only her pride was hurt when she realized how naive she had been.

PRIMARY AND SECONDARY VICTIMS

When we speak of victims of sex crimes, we are speaking of those people (primary victims) who have been psychologically and physically damaged by other persons who have perpetrated sexual attacks on them. But these are not the only victims—there are secondary victims also. These are the people who are close to the primary victims: fathers and mothers, husbands and wives, sisters and brothers, other relatives, and friends of those who have been victimized and, too often, murdered.

Hagan reports a typology of victims in terms of their degree of guilt in the perpetration of a crime:

(1) the *completely innocent victim,* such as a child or an unconscious person

(2) the *victim with minor guilt,* such as a woman who provokes a miscarriage and dies as a result

(3) the *victim as guilty as offender,* such as in the case of suicide and euthanasia

(4) the *victim as more guilty than the offender,* such as a person who provokes someone to commit a crime

(5) the *victim as most guilty,* such as an aggressor who is killed in self-defense

(6) the *simulating or imaginary victim,* such as paranoids, hysterics, or senile persons (Hagan, 1990: 217)

The overwhelming majority of victims of sex criminals must be viewed as completely innocent victims. These victims have not contributed to their own victimization.

This chapter is devoted to discussion of primary victims of sex criminals—completely innocent victims who have undergone serious and traumatic sexual ordeals such as rape, mutilation, murder, picquerism, and evisceration. The special needs and concerns of secondary victims are also discussed. In too many cases, sexual victimization leaves primary and secondary victims to their own limited financial and psychological resources.

BEING A VICTIM OF A SERIOUS SEXUAL CRIME

An issue that is immediately raised in the minds of many victims is, "What did I do to cause this?" Feelings of guilt, shame, and responsibility often cloud the issue that the victim is not to blame for the act that occurred. It is often the case that victims have in some way contributed to their own victimization, but this is not to say that these victims are somehow to blame. For example, a young woman certainly has the right to walk down a dark alley in the early morning hours. It might not be the wise thing to do, but she does have that right. A man in a bar certainly has the right to flash a large wad of bills. It might not be wise to do that, but he certainly has the right to do so. In neither of these cases is the person culpable for any victimization that could result from their actions.

However, many still seem to want to "blame the victim." In a northern state, a judge ruled that a man was not guilty of rape because the woman dressed in a "provocative" fashion. There are more than a few persons who believe the myth that women invite rape through the manner in which they dress or the way they act. Apparently this judge is one of those believers. Many victims undergo strong feelings of guilt related to their role in the crime. Some women also have accepted the mythology that women somehow invite the crime ("She deserves what she gets"; "She must have asked for it"; "She led him on.").

Another feeling expressed by many victims is that of fear. Pervasive fear can affect victims' perceptions about their world, their relationships, and their own self-images. When an attacker has victimized a person once, the victim can remain fearful for some time that the attacker knows where she lives, where she works, where she shops, and so on. This sense of fear is exacerbated if the perpetrator has vowed to return to victimize again. Fear as a cost of violent crime has personal, social, and economic consequences, as outlined by Sheley (1979):

Personal consequences: withdrawal and retreat. Whatever it is based on, fear of crime influences the thoughts and actions of many Americans. And most responses to this fear involve some form of social withdrawal. Various surveys reported by Sheley indicate that 43% of urban populations and 16% of the nation as a whole remains off the streets at night because a criminal attack is feared.

One out of ten carries a weapon for protection when going out at night. Regardless of the actual crime rate in their present community, as many as one of every five respondents in one study was influenced by his or her fear of victimization to consider moving to a new, "safer" residential area.

Social consequences: erosion of solidarity. . . . Sheley emphasizes that fear of crime is primarily fear of strangers. Unfortunately, the erosion of solidarity and social contact may increase the opportunities for criminals to perpetrate violent crimes on those who try actively to maintain their social participation. One point of caution, however, must be noted here. Information from a recent study . . . indicates "that fear of crime should not be viewed cavalierly as irrational or unjustified. For most population groups there is a high degree of correspondence between adjusted victimization rates and fear of crime." From this research, "it appears that any strategy to reduce fear will be unsuccessful if efforts to lower victimization rates are ignored."

Economic consequences: billions of dollars. Indirect costs flowing from fear of crime include the expenses connected with installation of alarm systems, hiring of security personnel, and acquisition of guns or other weapons for self-protection. Many other things could doubtless be added; the point is that problems of morale in the form of fears about violent crime flow essentially from the increased existence of such crime. In short, violent crime and especially homicide secondarily victimizes the community and society as well as the primary . . . victim. (pp. 15-16)

Feelings of hurt also accompany victimization. This affective sensation typically arises from the victim's not being able to understand why a person would be motivated to do such a thing. The pain here is turned inward. Anger is another effect, but anger is directed outward—this may be a better psychological reaction than hurt because the feeling is directed toward someone other than oneself.

DEALING WITH THE VICTIMIZATION

Reactions and adjustments to a sexual assault are often similar to those a person might experience following another life crisis. Of course, they vary in time, duration, frequency, and intensity from one person to another. They will also vary according to the support system the victim may have—family, religious, and social supports—as well as the type of attack.

There are particular phases of adjustment through which many victims pass. Those listed below are common, but they do vary from one victim to another, and there is no one "right" way to adjust.

- *Stage 1: shock.* During this period the victim may experience acute anxiety, pangs of guilt, episodes of fear. In this stage, many victims exhibit behavior that runs the gamut from hysteria to behavioral numbness.
- *Stage 2: denial.* During this period the victim may make a concentrated effort to put the entire episode of the sexual attack behind her. She may feel it is "time to forget" the attack. She may attempt to suppress the feelings that came to the psychological surface in Stage 1. She will probably discuss the attack as little as possible, and she will try to return to her regular daily routine.
- *Stage 3: integration.* Despite the psychological attempt at restoration, many victims discover that sexual attacks have more impact upon them than they initially realized. Nightmares, breakdowns in interpersonal relationships, employment difficulties, and the like often continue to be problems in the adjustment process.

From a psychological point of view it is important to move the victim from a position that the culpability rests with the victim herself and have her place the blame for the attack exactly where it belongs, on the perpetrator. There are several ways to do this. From an interpersonal point of view, while speaking with a sex crime victim one must allow her to express feelings in the way she finds most comfortable. It is vital for the victim to ventilate and talk out those feelings that concern her. Some of the distressing issues that may surface and that must be dealt with include the victim's fears about having contracted a disease in the attack, about death, about unwanted pregnancy resulting from the attack, about other persons discovering what happened, and about being victimized again.

The setting for this interview must also be considered. It must be private and secure from interruptions. Unwanted or clamorous persons must not be permitted to invade this physical or psychological space.

SOCIETY AND VICTIMS' RIGHTS GROUPS RESPONSES

In Louisville, Kentucky, two 16-year-old male high school students were abducted at gunpoint. Their bodies were found later that evening. Both boys had been bound, and one had been sodomized. Both had been shot in the head. Less than eight hours later, two men were arrested and charged with their murders. This horrendous crime was the impetus for the creation of a victims' rights group, Citizens and Victims for Justice Reform.

The Stephanie Roper Society was founded by her parents after this young college-aged woman was abducted beside her disabled car. She was taken to an abandoned house, where she was repeatedly raped, then burned and shot in the head. Her killers were apprehended within a week of the crime.

It is not surprising that organizations such as the two mentioned above have arisen in recent years to deal with the problems confronted by victims, both primary and secondary. These groups have often voiced their dissatisfaction with the operation of the criminal justice system and have offered a variety of services to victims of all types of crime, not only those that involve sex as a motivating factor.

This concern for victims' rights has emerged as one of the most significant issues in the last decade. Many states have compensation programs that have been initiated to help survivors of attacks and the families of murder victims. In Kentucky, for example, a victim may receive up to $25,000, but he or she must demonstrate evidence of financial need, report the crime to the police within two days of its occurrence, and file a claim within 12 months. It is difficult to see why the financial condition of the victim should play a role in deciding whether or not the victim is to be awarded some type of financial remuneration. Fortunately, 30 of the 44 states that have victim compensation programs do not insist that the victim show some type of financial need.

Many victims' rights programs include services such as the following:

- *personal advocacy:* helping victims receive all the services to which they are entitled by both social service and criminal justice agencies
- *referral:* recommending or obtaining assistance other than that given by the programs
- *restitution assistance:* urging judges to order, or probation authorities to collect, restitution, and helping violent crime victims fill out the proper papers necessary to receive compensation
- *court orientation:* helping victims and witnesses understand the criminal justice system and their participation in it
- *transportation:* providing victims with rides to and from court, to social service agencies, and, if necessary, to shelters
- *court escort:* escorting witnesses to court and staying with them during the proceedings

Samaha (1988, p. 94) reports that the emotional support victims' rights groups give to victims may indeed be their most important function.

CONSEQUENCES FOR SECONDARY VICTIMS

The consequences for secondary victims of sexual assaults may indeed be very dramatic. This is especially true when there is a homicide involved. Until recently, however, there has been little attention paid to the widespread secondary victimization that occurs because of such attacks. It has been estimated that about 5,000 victims annually fall prey to serial killers. If this is accurate, a large "data set" does indeed exist for serious empirical researchers to examine. A few studies have been conducted (Castleberry, 1982; Friedman et al., 1982; Lavrakas, 1981), but there appears to be a real scarcity of information regarding the consequences of sex crimes for other victims. Some of these consequences are discussed below.

Economic Consequences

Many victims are harmed or even murdered during their most productive years or when their productive years lie ahead. Some have families and other dependents who suffer great financial loss because of the sexual victimization. This is true not only of those who die as a result of a sexual assault, but also often of those who have suffered at the hands of a sexual offender and have not been able to reach their former or potential level of productivity. Lauder (1985) quotes one victim:

> The man who murdered my husband is in prison. . . . Taxpayers are paying for his room, board, and medical and psychiatric help. My husband was my only means of support. I'm now destitute, very ill, and have no financial means. Meanwhile, the murderer has 600 acres of valuable property. Why should the man who ruined my life be able to keep and return in a few years to that, while I have nothing? (p. 169)

According to Holmes and De Burger (1988, p. 143), there are issues of fairness in the matter of dealing with the needs of both primary and secondary victims, but the meeting of this fairness doctrine is somehow balanced with the financial resources that are available to address all of the financial and economic issues properly. Lauder (1985) offers a critique on the economic aspects of secondary victimizations:

(1) It is a travesty of justice that, while the costs of defense are often paid fully by tax funds, through a public defender service, victims or survivors in states without crime compensation laws get nothing.

(2) Federal laws should require that profits reaped by celebrated murderers from films, books, and so forth about their lives must be placed in a fund for restitution to survivors or the community. Only a small incentive amount should be excluded from this requirement.

(3) If states are willing to pay the bill for psychological or psychiatric counseling of the homicidal criminal, why are so few willing to foot the bill for counseling of the victim's surviving spouse or children?

(4) If states are willing to fund the extensive costs of defense counsel and related expenses for a perpetrator of homicidal violence, then they should also fund the costs of a survivor's suit for wrongful death against the convicted killer. In the event hidden assets are uncovered or the killer is paroled to productive work, payment of any award to the survivors would be enforceable by the court. (pp. 165-170)

Morale and Mental Health Consequences

The impact of sexual victimization on secondary victims can be great; it may indeed be fatal. Domestic problems, too often leading to marital dissolution or breakdowns in interpersonal relationships, are often the result of rape. In cases involving serial murder, the primary victims are often not found for weeks or months—sometimes even for years. Many are never found. This certainly has an impact upon the morale and the health, both mental and physical, of the secondary victims.

Consider the cases of four families of primary victims of Ted Bundy—the Aime, Kent, Naslund, and Hawkins families.[1] Laura Aime, an 18-year-old victim, was killed by Bundy in 1974. Her father was hospitalized for depression after Laura's death. There appears to be little doubt that his depression was at least exacerbated by the victimization of his daughter. As he stated as he drove by the mountain parkway, looking toward the spot where the police found Laura's body, "My little baby was up there all by herself and there was nothing I could do to help her" (author's files). Mr. Aime died in 1987 of heart problems, no doubt complicated by the stress of his daughter's death. A Mormon family, the Aimes found little consolation in their faith.

Belva Kent is the mother of Debbie Kent, who was murdered by Bundy in 1974. In a personal interview, Mrs. Kent said that Debbie's body has never been found, but that a kneecap had been found in 1989 that they believe belonged to Debbie. The Kents held a memorial service for Debbie alongside the headstone they erected for their daughter. Billy, Debbie's younger brother, was killed in an automobile accident in the mid-1980s. Mrs. Kent and her husband have since divorced. Mrs. Kent said that the media originally badgered her family, appearing interested only in selling newspapers and raising TV ratings. She said that the media actually believed that Debbie was a runaway and a troubled youngster, and would not consider the possibility of foul play until much later. However, as the case developed and time passed, Mrs. Kent believes the media have become more sensitive and appreciative of the feelings and emotions the survivors endure. Also devout Mormons, the Kent family found solace within their religion.

Denise Naslund's mother has not changed her daughter's bedroom since the day she went with her friends to Lake Sam in 1974. Constant concern about what her daughter had to go through on the day of her death is always on her mind.

The father of Georgeann Hawkins, another Bundy victim, stated, "You just want to reach out and do something. . . . But you can't. You get so drawn out. You waste so damn much emotional effort trying to transfer your hate and bitterness. You get over the loss, then you keep getting reminded of it" (Michaud & Aynesworth, 1983, p. 313).

These cases are not unusual. The mother of one of Jerry Brudos's victims, Mildred Slawson, stated that she was so upset with a book written about the serial killer and what the author said about the killing of her daughter that she went into the hospital for a week. Mrs. Slawson said that the author had never interviewed her about her daughter, a point about which she is quite bitter. She was additionally upset that the author of the book had access to police information that she, as the mother of a primary victim, was denied. In an interview, Karen Sprinker's mother also said that she disapproved of a book being written concerning the murder of her daughter. She was somewhat unnerved that an author could profit from a crime such as this, a fact that actually contributed to her grief as a secondary victim. She also suffered further because of hearing from others some of the content of the book, including what her daughter suffered before her death. She stated that she had not read the book, and ended the interview by asking, "Why do people write things like this?" These killings occurred in the late 1960s, but the pain persists in the minds of these secondary victims.

CONCLUSION

The victimization continues for survivors of sexual assault. Victimized again by social and law enforcement agencies intended to serve them, the primary and secondary victims are too often left to their own resources to cope with the consequences of their victimization. Many experience rudeness and impersonal treatment from bureaucrats who are supposed to be public servants. Too often they find no one who will come to their aid either formally or personally to help them with their suffering. They experience iatrogenic victimization (Holmes & De Burger, 1989, p. 145); that is, victimization caused by the process of dealing with the original victimization. This must cease. The establishment of self-help organizations and victims' rights groups, passage of strong and effective legislation, and active enforcement of such legislation are all steps toward making sure that neither primary nor secondary victims are again victimized.

Note

1. I would like to thank James Massie for the information used in this chapter regarding the families of Ted Bundy's and Jerry Brudos's victims.

10

Treatment of Sex Offenders

There is less than enthusiastic endorsement regarding the treatment and rehabilitation of sex offenders. As much as 25-30% of a prison population is made up of these offenders; the numbers themselves pose monumental problems for security as well as for treatment. These incarcerated offenders form a group that is quite heterogeneous (Welch, 1988). They come from backgrounds that reflect all socioeconomic classes; some are aggressive, some are not. Although many ages, marital statuses, and races are represented, most are in their 20s and 30s, many are married, and they are predominantly white.

Professional corrections has moved from an early philosophical position of retribution and revenge to one of rehabilitation and reintegration. Evolving from the harsh treatment found in prisons in the early history of this country, corrections and the various treatment modalities have strived for a synthesis of humane treatment and personality change for the protection of society as well as the betterment of the individual.

The emphasis on reform, restraint, congregate workplaces, the "medical model," and finally community-based treatment programs have all generated input into the issue of what to do with sex offenders. There are social as well as financial factors that affect the operation of a treatment program not only in a prison setting but also in other types of correctional facilities as well as in the private sector. These factors must be addressed for a treatment program not only to survive but to be effective.

No unanimous agreement has been reached concerning the best direction to proceed. Only one majority agreement can be reached: Society must be protected. If change occurs within the personality of the offender, this is well and good, but above all society must be protected. But how does this occur? Either the sex criminal must be locked away for the rest of his life or change must happen—the sex criminal must be "treated" and "rehabilitated."

WHAT IS TREATMENT?

Rehabilitation is often mistaken to be synonymous with treatment. This is not the case. *Treatment* is an action word; treatment entails processes carried out so that rehabilitation can be realized. *Rehabilitation* is a result of a process of treatment. It is indeed a noble effort to effect rehabilitation for everyone. There are some, however, who would argue that there are persons who are not amenable to the process of treatment. For example, Rizzo (1981) states, "It is my conviction that there are persons beyond the scope and reach of modern behavioral sciences' ability to rehabilitate" (p. 45). And Welch (1988) has said, "No responsible person would say that we cure sex offenders. . . . We give them the tools to control their deviance" (p. 7).

There is also a problem with the word *rehabilitate*. In the medical sense, rehabilitation may be what we wish to accomplish with the sex offender, but the medical model has lost a great deal of its luster in only the past few years. We do not want simply to "make" the person what he used to be; we want to change him so he will not become as he was. *Habilitation*, then, might be the better word. However, since *rehabilitation* is the commonly used term, and since we now know the difference between rehabilitation and habilitation, I will continue to use rehabilitation here.

In rehabilitating sex offenders, one item that must be kept in mind is that not all sex criminals are alike. The National Institute of Corrections has designed a typology of sex offenders:

(1) first offenders with no previous record who blame their offense on stress of substance abuse

(2) controlled chronic offenders, who are the most calculating and antisocial, and whose crimes are increasing in severity and frequency

(3) a group of chronic offenders who are inept, possibly mentally slow, and impulsive (Welch, 1988, p. 7)

REHABILITATION AND RECIDIVISM

The literature regarding the success of various types of treatment programs, modalities, and facilities is typically contradictory. In an older study by Sturup (1968), sex offenders seldom were reported to having committed new sex crimes and were considered not to be a danger to themselves or others. This same generalization was supported by the research of Amir (1971), Groth, Longo, and McFadin (1982) and Tappan (1971).

It is often apparent that some treatment programs are more effective than others. At the Oregon State Hospital, for example, the rate of recidivism for sex offenders over a 6-year period was 10-14%. At the Western State Hospital in Washington, the rate of recidivism over a 17-year period was 28.7%. Does this mean that the Oregon State Hospital program is better than the one in Washington? Not necessarily. Many details affect the final success rate of a program; these details can differ widely. The time frame that is used to measure the rate of success as well as type of offense committed are two considerations in the measurement of recidivism. Success may be measured by whether the subject reoffends by committing another sex crime or by committing any type of crime, sexual or not—this clearly will influence the measured rate of recidivism. Controlling intake is another method of influencing the rate of success. If a program admits only minor sex criminals, that program's chances of having a high long-term success rate are better than if the program admits more hard-core offenders.

Romero and Williams (1985) studied 231 adult males who were exhibitionists, pedophiles, or sexual assaulters. They found that exhibitionists were arrested on sex-related offenses twice as often as were sexual assaulters. Sexual assaulters were found to have committed as many nonsexual offenses as sexual offenses. The crimes of the sexual assaulters (rapists) were usually linked with an overall pattern of violent behavior. Exhibitionists and pedophiles studied had lower rates of nonsex crimes and higher rates of sex crimes than did the sexual assaulters. In their conclusion, Romero and Williams call for long-term analysis of the recidivism rate of sex offenders and the discovery of undetected crimes, both sex crimes and nonsex crimes.

OBSTACLES TO TREATMENT

In dealing with sex offenders, there are many barriers to rehabilitation. Many legislators and citizens are concerned that sex criminals are "coddled," and that too much tax money is spent on these undeserving individuals. Others believe that incapacitation is the answer, and that any type of treatment program is a total waste of time. The impediments to effective treatment fall into three broad categories: societal obstacles, political obstacles, and criminal justice system obstacles.

Societal Obstacles

There is a general belief in society that people are to be held personally responsible for their own actions. This appears to be a return to the "classical school of criminology," in which individuals are considered to have free will and deterrence to crime is gained through swift, sure, and public punishment. Many believe that treatment programs designed for the rehabilitation of sex offenders constitute an unrealistic approach. The real answer lies in punishment, including incapacitation of the offenders and demand for retribution (Fogel, 1975; Irwin, 1988). According to this view, treatment programs do not belong inside prison walls, and therapy should be extended only to those persons who are able to pay on their own once they have "paid their debt to society."

Societal rejection of sex offenders creates low status for such offenders and a negative treatment environment in prison (see Figure 10.1). Society is reluctant to appropriate funds for the treatment of persons who perpetrate such despicable crimes (Vaughn & Sapp, 1989). When an increase in funds for such treatment is realized, it typically goes into community-based treatment programs (Cox, 1984) rather than prison programs. Because of this pervasive attitude, in-prison rehabilitation may not be a viable process for changing the lives of many sex offenders.

Political Obstacles

With too many politicians, it seems that the main concern is reelection. Reflecting the main concerns of their constituents, politicians who are judged to be "soft on crime" certainly run a great risk at election time. Maintaining a hard line against sex criminals almost ensures a popular response from the voters. But this may have a deleterious effect on fiscal maintenance for programs in institutions as well as community-based treatment programs.

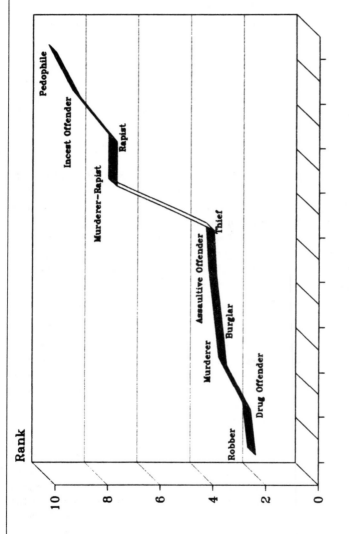

Figure 10.1. Correctional Institution Status Hierarchy
SOURCE: Adapted from Vaughn and Sapp (1989).

Financial maintenance almost ensures viability of a program, and such maintenance requires legislative support. If an elected member of state or federal government has an ill-deserved reputation for being "soft on crime" because he or she has voted in support of treatment programs for sex criminals, this may become an insurmountable problem at reelection.

Criminal Justice System Obstacles

The criminal justice system has the main responsibility for the treatment of sex criminals. However, with the swing back to custody and incapacitation, it appears that treatment and rehabilitation are again taking a backseat. It is true that almost every penal institution has some type of treatment program, and some are more advanced than others, but the reality of most institutions is custody.

Jails do not offer treatment as such, although some maintain psychologists or social workers on staff. This is probably just as well because of the short time the sex criminal is usually in the jail setting. Prisons, however, do offer treatment, although the quality of that treatment can be questionable. In prisons, just as the turnover rate of security personnel is extremely high, so is that of treatment personnel. Salaries for treatment personnel are often so low that they fall below the poverty line for a person with a family of four. In Kentucky, for example, a correctional officer with a spouse and two children is qualified for food stamps. This is hardly an incentive for dedicated and professionally prepared persons to stay on the job.

The professional administrator in a prison may find it very difficult to allocate resources, both human resources and financial support, to administer a sex offenders' treatment program. Because of the low status of sex offenders and their likelihood of being victimized by other inmates, they are often segregated from the general prison population; this segregation further isolates sex criminals and limits their treatment participation and personal movement (Cotton & Groth, 1982).

The clients themselves often pose serious obstacles to the treatment process. Sex offenders have gone about their business on the outside by being manipulative and thwarting attempts at change. They naturally bring these attitudes into the therapeutic situation, and this certainly impedes the process of attempted change. Sex offenders are typically viewed as being at the bottom of the hierarchy of prison inmates (Akerstrom, 1986), and this status may pose a further impediment, as many sex offenders are reluctant to identify themselves as such because of the ramifications this may have in their dealings with others inside the prison walls.

So inside the system itself, the problems are manifested on all levels: the administration, the custody staff, the treatment personnel, and the sex offender. The criminal justice system itself must now decide what course it will take with this very serious problem. The criminal justice system's relationship to state and national government leaders is crucial; as that leadership can change every four years, program stability is an ongoing concern.

TYPES OF TREATMENT

Just as there are different types of sex criminals, there are different forms of treatment directed toward the resolution and change of the sex criminal personality. These treatment programs (therapies) usually fall into one of three types: behavioral, cognitive, or medical.

Behavioral Therapy

Behavioral therapies typically utilize rewards and punishments to influence client behavior. In sexual counseling, the rewards and punishments are used to change sexual patterns and scripts of behavior. In one treatment therapy, for example, a sex offender may be shown slides of erotic scenes while his extent of physical and psychological arousal is monitored by a penile plethysmograph; when he begins to become aroused by the materials, he may receive negative reinforcement in the form of a dose of ammonia administered through plastic tubing fastened under his nose. Other methods of behavior modification may include encouraging the offender to talk about his favorite sexual fantasy and then administering ammonia if he becomes sexually aroused by his "deviant fantasy."

Cognitive Therapy

In this approach a sex offender is encouraged to change his basic perceptions of his own sex life and the world around him as it pertains to sex and his interactions with others. These perceptions typically revolve around sex, education, skills, relationships, and so on. Through instruction, an attempt is made to help the offender relearn the world and his roles as they interact with the world. For example, the offender is taught skills that will help him appropriately express not only affection but anger and hostility.

> Offenders may re-enact their crimes on video, then show those videos to their group and to their spouse and outside friends. In an attempt to teach them empathy, they will read books and see videos from the victim's point of view, and perhaps meet with the victims or victims' counselors, or write letters to their own victims. (Welch, 1988, p. 9)

In this approach the offender is taught to recognize the steps or stages that have led him to commit his crimes. By becoming aware of his own personal "danger signs" he may be able to divert himself from situations that in the past would result in some type of sexual victimization.

Medical Therapy

Medical programs typically use drugs, such as Depo-Provera, to lower sex criminals' testosterone levels. It is believed that the manifestation of sexual aggression is based in some type of hormonal imbalance. The administration of the drug does not alter the sexual preference of the offender, but it does decrease his physical urges to act them out and makes it easier for him to control those urges (Melella, Travin, & Cullen, 1989, p. 224).

Depo-Provera was initiated as a drug of treatment for sex offenders in 1966 at Johns Hopkins University (Bradford, 1983). It is a synthetic progestin that inhibits the release of androgen, a male hormone, from the testicles. After stopping the administration of the drug, erectile and ejaculatory capacity usually begin to return within 7 to 10 days (Callan, 1985, p. 6).

It may be that Depo-Provera is best suited for those sex criminals for whom fantasy plays a preoccupational role: pedophiles, exhibitionists, and voyeurs. The use of Depo-Provera is controversial. There are some indications that long-term effects may include diabetes, gallstones, thrombosis, and possibly cancer. Short-term effects may include deep depression, high blood pressure, dramatic weight gain, and fatigue (Callan, 1985). In addition, there are some who believe that treating very dangerous sex offenders—such as rapists—with a drug does not alter the rage and anger these individuals have; there is some fear that they may express these feelings by committing other forms of fatal physical violence. It is also believed that this type of therapy should be used only in a secure setting, such as a prison or a hospital.

TREATMENT IN THE COMMUNITY

Because more than 98% of all individuals sent to prison someday return to society as free persons, steps must be taken to do what can be done to make society safe. One such step is mandatory treatment programs for sex offenders.

After release from a correctional facility, sex offenders, like other ex-convicts, need structure and security. In prison, an individual's daily activities are carefully structured; inmates make few decisions for themselves. On the outside, however, decisions have to be made continually: when to get up, when to go to bed, what and when to eat, what to wear, and so on. The released sex offender's decision to seek treatment, and to stay in the program, is critical.

Emerging environmental opportunities make themselves available to sex criminals. Careful attention must be directed toward making the released sex offender aware of the various personal danger signs that may lead him back to the actions of a sex criminal—preoccupation with deviant sexual fantasies or with particular types of pornography, cruising certain areas to look for victims, and experiencing stress in personal, business, or other relationships. Released sex offenders must be careful about placing themselves in high-risk situations. For example, a pedophile must not place himself in a situation where he may have unlimited access to children without some type of supervision. An exhibitionist with a fantasy about young girls must be careful about placing himself in situations where he is sure to come into contact with young girls.

CONCLUSION

There is growing concern about the protection of society from those persons who present a clear and present danger to its law-abiding members. Incapacitation may be an answer, but it is only a short-term answer. The changing of the sex offender's sexual value system and propensity for violence directed toward others must be dealt with. Also, we must learn more about early identification of those persons who may become sexually violent as they age into adulthood. There is no doubt that protection is a right; the issue becomes how to accomplish it. We must give serious consideration to identification, isolation, and effective change of those who are dangerous.

Glossary

abnormal sex
> generic term encompassing all criminalized or disvalued sexual behaviors, with the exceptions of adultery and fornication

adultery
> sexual intercourse between a man and a woman at least one of whom is married but not to the other

age of consent
> statutory age, differing from one jurisdiction to another, at which an individual is considered legally able to consent to having sexual relations

algolagnia
> sexual satisfaction derived from the anticipation of inflicting or suffering pain; a manifestation of sadomasochism

ambisexual
> bisexual

anal eroticism

sexual behavior focusing on the anus; includes oral-anal contacts (rimming), insertion of the penis into the anus (sodomy), digital insertion into the anus, sexual stimulation by anal odors

analism

preoccupation with the anus as a focus of sexual satisfaction

anaphrodisiac

a chemical preparation supposed to reduce or eliminate sexual erection in the male

androgynous

possessing both male and female primary and/or secondary sex characteristics

anthropophagy

cannibalism; sexual satisfaction received from the eating of the flesh or drinking of the blood of a victim

aphrodisiac

a chemical substance supposed to stimulate sex interest and capability

aquaeroticism

sexual gratification received from placing the head or the entire body in water so as to produce a sensation of losing consciousness during orgasm

autoeroticism

masturbation and other forms of self-gratification

auto-monosexual perversion

sexual actions performed on or with one's own body (e.g., self-fellatio, self-abuse, self-mutilation)

autosexuality

perversions performed on oneself, including self-fellation and sadomasochistic practices; also includes masturbation

bathroom phobia

toilet phobia; fear of falling into the toilet or fear of monster coming from the toilet to attack one's genitals; said to be present in male anal erotics

bestiality

sexual contacts between human beings and animals

bisexual

engaging in or interested in both heterosexual and homosexual behaviors

brachioproticism

insertion of the arm into the rectum of another person for sexual pleasure; brachioprotic eroticism

buggery

anal sodomy

castration

surgical excision of the male testes

catamite

homosexual prostitute or kept male

chicken

young male, usually in adolescence, who makes himself available for sexual acts with older male partners, generally for money

chicken hawk

older male who pursues young males for sexual purposes

child molester

one who seeks sexual satisfaction with young children

circle jerk

group masturbation

clap

gonorrhea

clitoridectomy

surgical removal of all or part of the clitoris

coitus interruptus

coitus in which the penis is withdrawn from the vagina before ejaculation

community standard

phrase used by the U.S. Supreme Court in the *Miller* (1973) decision in defining material as pornographic and subject to criminal sanction if patently offensive in a given geographical area

consensual acts

generic term covering acts between two or more persons that take place by mutual consent, with no threat or use of force, usually restricted to acts between adults

consolateur

dildo; penis-shaped object utilized by females in autoerotic practices or lesbian activities

coprolagnia

sexual satisfaction received from handling, smelling, or eating feces

coprophagia

sexual satisfaction received from watching others evacuate the bowels or bladder; being urinated upon; may also include writing graffiti on bathroom walls

coprophilia

sexual satisfaction received from saying or listening to sexual or obscene language

coprophobia

fear of excreting or excreta

copulatio analis
pederasty, anal sodomy

corneali complex
incestuous desire of a mother for her son

cross-dressing
transvestism

cruising
seeking strangers for a sexual encounter (term usually restricted to homo-sexuals)

cunnilingus
oral contact with the female genitalia

dildo
artificial penis

dimorphism
having both male and female anatomical parts, sexual characteristics, or responses

emasculate
asexualize, castrate

eonism
transvestism; cross-dressing

erogenous zones
areas of the body particularly sensitive to sexual stimulation

erotic hanging
a form of autoeroticism in which sexual gratification is received from pressure placed on the arteries in the neck, resulting in lightheadedness; often results in accidental death

erotographomania

conduct in which major sexual satisfaction is derived from viewing explicit paintings, sculpture, or other objects

erotolalia

deriving major sexual satisfaction from talking about or listening to talk about sex

erotomani

a compulsive interest in sexual matters

erotophile

one with a strong interest in and concentration on erotic matters

erotophobic

afraid of sex; hostile to evidence of sexuality

exhibitionism

the act of deliberate exposing of oneself

exhibitionist

one receiving sexual gratification from the deliberate exposure of private body parts in inappropriate situations

extracoital

sexual connection between male and female not involving penetration of the vagina; may be oral, anal, intermammary, interfemoral, or other

fellatio

taking the penis into the mouth (recipient may be either male or female)

fellator

male insertee in fellatio

fellatrix

female insertee in fellatio

fetish

an inanimate object to which sexual feelings are attached

flagellation

a form of sadomasochism in which sexual satisfaction is obtained from whipping or being whipped

flagellationism

an intense desire to beat, whip, or club someone

flasher

exhibitionist

formicophilia

sexual arousal linked with insects or other small creatures crawling on body parts

fornication

sexual intercourse between a man and a woman, neither of whom is married

frigidity

inability to respond to sexual stimulation

frottage

receiving sexual satisfaction from rubbing up against the body parts of another

frotteur

one who practices frottage

gerontophilia

abnormal desire of a younger person for sexual relations with a much older male or female; also known as gerontosexuality

golden shower

urolagnia; urinating upon or being urinated upon by another to receive sexual satisfaction *gonorrhea*

venereal disease characterized in males by an emission from the penis

hebephile

a pedophile interested in young children from puberty to adolescence

heterosexuality

sex drive oriented toward gratification with the other sex

homoerotophobia

fear of being considered homosexual, also fear of homosexuality

homophile

homosexual

homosexuality

sex drive oriented toward gratification with the same sex

homosociality

intimate but not necessarily sexual social relationship between persons of the same gender

hypersexuality

state of being oversexed; nymphomania (female), satyriasis (male)

incest

sexual relations between persons who are too closely related by blood to marry

indecent exposure

exhibitionism

infantosexuality

focus of sexual desire on very young (prepubertal) children

infibulation

self-torture of the genitals

interfemoral coitus

placement of the penis between the thighs of a partner to effect ejaculation by friction

intermammary coitus

placement of the penis between the breasts of a partner to effect ejaculation by friction

interversion

term formerly used for homosexuality

irrumation fellatio klismaphilia

sexual arousal linked with the receiving or administration of enemas

lesbianism

female homosexuality

lewd

legal term used to describe criminal, depraved, disvalued, and perverse sexual behaviors

libido

sexual drive

lust murder

murder for sexual reasons

masochism

receiving sexual gratification from having pain inflicted on oneself

masturbation

stimulation of the genitalia to produce sexual gratification

misogynist

one who hates women

mixoscopia

> deriving sexual satisfaction from watching other persons engage in sexual activity; a form of triolism

mysoped

> aggressive and sadistic child offender

mysophilia

> sexual gratification associated with filth

narratophilia

> receiving sexual gratification or stimulation from listening to sexual stories; term may apply to passive partner in obscene telephone calls

necrophilia

> erotic interest in dead bodies

necrosadism

> interest in having sex with dead bodies; necrosadistic killers murder to have sex with the dead

nymphomania

> compulsive, excessive desire for sexual intercourse in the female

obscene phone sex

> receiving sexual satisfaction from the use of the telephone in sexual themes

obscenity

> anything disgusting to the senses; may or may not have anything to do with sex

onanism

> masturbation; also another term for coitus interruptus

oral eroticism

> fellatio, cunnilingus, rimming

oralism
oral eroticism

paraphilia
classification of sexual behaviors, some of which may be considered aberrant

partialism
attaching sexual feelings to isolated parts of the body

pederasty
male pedophile interested in having anal sex with young boys

pedomania
intense, compulsive sexual interest in young children

pedophilia
sexual attraction of adults to young children

penilingus
fellatio

pictophilia
deriving sexual satisfaction from erotic pictures

polyandry
one woman having two or more husbands at the same time

polygamy
plural spouses

polygyny
one man having two or more wives at the same time

pornography
anything made (written, photographed, drawn, or whatever) deliberately to arouse erotic feelings

pyromania

sexual gratification received from setting fires, watching smoke and flames, and so on; pathological fire setting

rape

forcible sexual penetration of an unwilling victim

rimming

oral-anal contact

sadism

sexual gratification received from the punishment of another person

saliromania

destruction or defilement of female undergarments or nude statues or paintings of females

sapphism

lesbianism

satyriasis

compulsive, excessive desire for sexual intercourse in the male

scatolophilia

receiving sexual satisfaction from making obscene telephone calls

scoptophilia

receiving sexual satisfaction from viewing the sexual organs of another

sex change

reassignment of gender; transsexualism

sex murder

lust murder

sexhibitionism
   obtaining sexual satisfaction from performing sex acts in front of an audience

sexual assault
   forced sexual attack upon an unwilling victim

sexual psychopath
   sex offender with psychopathic mentality

short eyes
   prison term for child sex offenders

sodomy
   sexual penetration of any orifice other than the vagina

statuophilia
   sexual love of statues or similar inanimate objects

swinging
   exchange of married partners for sexual purposes; mate swapping

syphilis
   a venereal disease

syphilophobia
   exaggerated fear of contracting a venereal disease

toucher
   frotteur

transsexual
   a person who is biologically one sex and psychologically the other

transvestism
   eonism; cross-dressing

transvestite

> one who practices transvestism

triolism

> receiving sexual satisfaction from seeing oneself and others in sexual scenes

undinism

> sexual attraction to urine

urophilia

> sexual attraction to urine

vampirism

> receiving sexual gratification from the smelling or drinking of blood

voyeur

> one who receives sexual gratification from viewing typically sexual scenes; Peeping Tom

zooerasty

> zooeroticism

zooeroticism

> sexual gratification achieved with animals, by stroking, petting, or kissing them, but not actual intercourse

zoophilia

> zooeroticism

zoosadism

> sexual gratification received from the killing or torturing of animals

References

Abel, G. (1981, April 15). *The evaluation of sexual offenders and their victims*. Paper presented at the St. Vincent Hospital and Medical Center, Portland, OR.

Abel, G., et al. (1988). Multiple paraphiliac diagnoses among sex offenders. *Bulletin of the American Academy of Psychiatry and the Law, 2*(2), 153-168.

Abraham, S., Hill, R., Orlofsky, S., Sass, L., & Sobel, L. (1980). *Pornography, obscenity and the law*. New York: Facts on File.

Akerstrom, M. (1986). Outcases in prison: The cases of informers and sex offenders. *Deviant Behavior, 7*(1), 1-20.

Allen, D. (1980). Young male prostitutes: A psychosocial study. *Archives of Sexual Behavior, 9*, 399-426.

American Psychiatric Association. (1987). *Desk reference to the criteria from DSM-III-R*. Washington, DC: Author.

Amir, M. (1971). *Patterns in forcible rape*. New York: Harcourt, Brace & World.

Ammons, C., & Ammons, R. (1987, October). [Research note]. *Psychological Reports, 60*, 153-159.

Araji, S., & Finkelhor, D. (1985). Explanations of pedophilia: Review of empirical research. *Bulletin of the American Academy of Psychiatry and Law, 13*(1), 17-36.

Attorney General's Office. (1986). *Attorney General's Commission report on pornography*. Washington, DC: Author.

Avery, C., & Johannis, T. (1985). *Love and marriage*. New York: Harcourt Brace Jovanovich.

Bahlmann, D., & Thomas, H. (1979). *Children and youth as victims of violence*. Paper presented at the Sixth National Conference on Juvenile Justice, Reno, NV.

129

Baker, A., & Duncan, S. (1985). Child sexual abuse: A study of prevalence in Great Britain. *Child Abuse and Neglect, 9*, 457-467.

Baker, C. (1978). Preying on playgrounds: The sexploitation of children in pornography and prostitution. *Pepperdine Law Review, 5*, 809-846.

Baker, R. (1983). Some considerations arising from the treatment of a patient with necrophilic fantasies in late adolescence and young adulthood. *Revista de Psicoanalisis, 40*(1), 157-173.

Barlow, H. (1990). *Introduction to criminology* (5th ed.). Glenview, IL: Scott, Foresman.

Barry, R. (1984). Incest: The last taboo, parts I and II. *FBI Law Enforcement Bulletin, 53*, 1-9, 15-19.

Bartholomew, A., Milte, K., & Galbally, F. (1978). Homosexual necrophilia. *Medicine, Science and the Law, 18*(1), 29-35.

Bartol, C. (1986). *Criminal behavior*. New York: Simon & Schuster.

Bell, A., & Weinberg, M. (1978). *Homosexualities: A study of diversities among men and women*. New York: Simon & Schuster.

Bell, A., Weinberg, M., & Hammersmith, S. (1981). *Sexual preference: Its development in men and women*. Bloomington: Indiana University Press.

Benward, J., & Densen-Gerber, J. (1975). Incest as a causative factor in antisocial behavior: An exploratory study. *Contemporary Drug Problems, 4*, 323-340.

Bieber, L., Dain, H., Dince, P., Drelich, M., Grand, H., Gunlach, R., Kremer, M., Rifkin, A., Wilbur, C., & Bieber, T. (1962). *Homosexuality*. New York: Vintage.

Blundell, B. (1983). *The world's most infamous murderers*. New York: Berkeley.

Bopp, W. (1987). *Crimes against women*. Springfield, IL: Charles C Thomas.

Bourgeois, M. (1983). Genital self-mutilation in humans. *Annales Medico-Psychologiques, 141*, 522-532.

Bourget, D., & Bradford, J. (1987). Fire fetishism, diagnostic and clinical implications: A review of two cases. *Canadian Journal of Psychiatry, 32*(6), 459-462.

Bowman, H. (1985). *Marriage for moderns* (7th ed.). New York: McGraw-Hill.

Bradford, J. (1983). The hormonal treatment of sexual offenders. *Bulletin of American Academy of Psychiatry and Law, 11*, 159-166.

Briere, J. (1989). University males' sexual interest in children: Predicting potential indices of "pedophilia" in a nonforensic sample. *Child Abuse and Neglect, 13*, 65-75.

Brill, A. (1941). Necrophilia. *Journal of Criminal Psychopathology, 2*, 51-73, 433-443.

Brownmiller, S. (1975). *Against our will: Men, women, and rape*. New York: Simon & Schuster.

Bullough, V. (1988). Historical perspective. *Journal of Social Work and Human Sexuality, 7*(1), 15-24.

Burdiit, T. (1978). *Social abuse of children and adolescents*. Houston: Texas Legislature, House Select Committee on Child Pornography.

Burg, B. (1982). The sick and the dead: The development of psychological theory on necrophilia from Krafft-Ebing to the present. *Journal of the History of the Behavioral Sciences, 218*, 242-254.

Burg, B. (1983). *Sodomy and the perception of evil*. New York: New York University Press.

Burgess, A., & Hazelwood, R. (1983). Autoerotic asphyxial deaths and social network response. *Journal of the American Orthopsychiatric Association, 53*(1), 166-170.

Burgess, A., Holstrom, L., Sgroi, S., & Groth, S. (1978). *Sexual assault of children and adolescents*. Lexington, MA: D. C. Heath.

Calef, V., & Weinshel, E. (1972). On certain equivalents of necrophilia. *International Journal of Psychoanalysis, 53*(1), 67-75.

Callan, J. (1985). Depo-Provera for sex offenders. *Corrections Compendium, 5*(2), 6-8.
Cameron, P. (1988). Did the American Psychological Association misrepresent scientific material to the U.S. Supreme Court? *Psychological Reports, 63,* 255-270.
Campbell, R. (1989). *Psychiatric dictionary.* New York: Oxford University Press.
Carrier, J. (1989). Society's view of homosexuality and bisexuality. *Journal of Homosexuality, 17,* 226-229.
Castleberry, V. (1982, August 1). The pain of survival. *Dallas Times Herald,* pp. 1, 6, 7.
Cavaiola, A., & Schiff, M. (1989). Self-esteem in abused chemically dependent adolescents. *Child Abuse and Neglect, 13,* 327-334.
Cesnik, J., & Coleman, E. (1989). Use of lithium carbonate in the treatment of autoasphyxia. *American Journal of Psychotherapy, 43,* 277-286.
Chesser, E. (1971). *Strange loves: The human aspects of sexual deviation.* New York: William Morrow.
Coleman, E. (1989). The development of male prostitution activity among gay and bisexual adolescents. *Journal of Homosexuality, 17,* 131-149.
Conacher, G., & Westwood, G. (1987). Infibulation. *British Journal of Psychiatry, 150,* 565-566.
Condy, R., Templer, D., Brown, R., & Veaco, L. (1987). Parameters of sexual contacts of boys and women. *Archives of Sexual Behavior, 16,* 379-394.
Conklin, J. (1989). *Criminology* (3rd ed.). New York: Macmillan.
Cooper, A., & Sacks, F. (1986). *The personality disorders and neurosis.* New York: Basic Books.
Cory, D., & LeRoy, J. (1963). *The homosexual and his society: A view from within.* New York: Citadel.
Cotton, D., & Groth, A. (1982). Inmate rape: Prevention and intervention. *Journal of Prison and Jail Health, 59*(2), 47-57.
Cox, D., & Maletsky, B. (1980). Victims of exhibitionism. In D. J. Cox & R. J. Daitzman (Eds.), *Exhibitionism* (pp. 289-293). New York: Garland.
Cox, G. (1984). Values, culture, and prison policy. *Prison Journal, 15,* 22-27.
Crew, L. (1986). *The gay academic.* New York: Etc.
Crewdson, J. (1988). *By silence betrayed.* Boston: Little, Brown.
Crime scene and profile characteristics of organized and disorganized murderers. (1985). *FBI Law Enforcement Bulletin, 54*(8), 18-25.
Crooks, R., & Baur, K. (1983). *Our sexuality.* Menlo Park, CA: Benjamin/Cummings.
Crossley, T., & Guzman, R. (1985). The relationship between arson and pyromania. *American Journal of Forensic Psychology, 3*(1), 39-44.
Dalby, J. (1988). Is telephone scatologia a variant of exhibitionism? *International Journal of Offender Therapy and Comparative Criminology, 32*(1), 45-49.
Dannemeyer, W. (1988). Our house (banning dial-a-porn). *National Review, 409,* 32.
Denko, J. (1973). Klismaphilia: Enema as a sexual preference. *American Journal of Psychotherapy, 27,* 232-250.
Denko, J. (1976). Klismaphilia: Application of the erotic enema deviance. *American Journal of Psychotherapy, 30,* 236-255.
Dense, R. (1982). Undinism: The fetishization of urine. *Canadian Journal of Psychiatry, 27,* 336-338.
Densen-Gerber, J., & Hutchison, S. (1978). *Medico-legal and societal problems involving children, child prostitution, child pornography and drug-related abuse.* Baltimore: University Park Press.
DeRiver, J. (1956). *The sexual criminal.* Springfield, IL: Charles C Thomas.

Dewaraja, R. (1987). Formicophilia, an usual paraphilia, treated with counseling and behavior therapy. *American Journal of Psychotherapy, 61*, 593-597.

Dewaraja, R., & Money, J. (1986). Transcultural sexology: Formicophilia, a newly named paraphilia in a young Buddhist male. *Sex and Marital Therapy, 2*, 593-597.

DeYoung, M. (1989). The world according to NAMBLA: Accounting for deviance. *Journal of Sociology and Social Welfare, 16*(1), 111-126.

Dixon, D. (1985). Perceived sexual satisfaction and marital happiness of bisexual and heterosexual swinging husbands. *Journal of Homosexuality, 11*, 209-222.

Dixon, J. (1985). The commencement of bisexual activity in swinging married women over age thirty. *Journal of Sex Research, 11*, 115-124.

Donnerstein, E., Linz, D., & Penrod, S. (1987). *Question of pornography: Research findings and policy implications*. New York: Free Press.

Dover, K. (1986). *Greek homosexuality*. Cambridge, MA: Harvard University Press.

Dwyer, M. (1988). Exhibitionism/voyeurism. *Journal of Social Work and Human Sexuality, 7*(1), 101-112.

Ebomoyi, E. (1987). Prevalence of female circumcision in two Nigerian communities. *Sex Roles, 17*, 31-38.

Ellis, A. (1986). *The encyclopedia of sexual behavior* (2nd ed.). New York: Hawthorne.

Ellis, A., & Abarbanel, A. (1967). *Sexual behavior*. New York: Hawthorne.

Ellis, A., & Abarbanel, A. (1973). *The encyclopedia of sexual behavior*. New York: Jason Aronson.

Ellis, H. (1946). *Psychology of sex: A manual for students*. New York: Emerson.

Estrich, S. (1987). *Real rape*. Cambridge, MA: Harvard University Press.

Faguet, R. (1980). Munchausen syndrome and necrophilia. *Suicide and Life-Threatening Behavior, 10*(4), 214-218.

Fang, B. (1976). Swinging: In retrospect. *Journal of Sex Research, 12*, 220-237.

Favazza, A. (1989). Infibulation. *Community Psychiatry, 40*(2), 137-145.

FBI Law Enforcement Bulletin (1985). *Crime Scene and Profile Characteristics of Organized and Disorganized Murderers, 54*, 18-25.

Finkelhor, D., & Araji, S. (1986). Explanations of pedophilia: A four factor model. *Journal of Sex Research, 22*, 145-161.

Fisch, R. (1987). Genital self-mutilation in males: Psychodynamic anatomy of a psychosis. *American Journal of Psychotherapy, 31*, 453-458.

Fishbach, S., & Malamuth, N. (1978). Sex and aggression: Proving the link. *Psychology Today, 12*, 111-122.

Fisher, B., Weisberg, D., & Marotta, T. (1982). *Report on adolescent male prostitution*. San Francisco: Urban and Rural System Associates.

Foerster, K., Foerster, G., & Roth, E. (1976). Necrophilia in a 17 year old girl. *Schweizer Archiv für Neurologie Neurochirurgie und Psychiatrie, 199*(1), 97-107.

Fogel, D. (1975). *We are the living proof*. Cincinnati: Anderson.

Freire, Arteta, B. (1981). The necrophiliac character according to Erich Fromm: The case of Amanda. *Psiquis: Revista de Psiquiartria, Psicologia y Psicosomatica, 2*(1), 23-32.

Freund, K., & Blanchard, R. (1986). The concept of courtship disorder. *Journal of Sex and Marital Therapy, 12*(2), 79-92.

Friedman, K., et al. (1982). *Victims and helpers: Reactions to crime*. Washington, DC: National Institute on Crime.

Fritz, G., Stoll, K., & Wagner, N. (1981). A comparison of males and females who were sexually molested as children. *Journal of Sex and Marital Therapy, 7*, 54-59.

Gallo, P. (1986). Views of future health workers in Somolia on female circumcision. *Medical Anthropology Quarterly, 17*, 32-36.

Gardner, T. (1989). *Criminal law: Principles and cases.* St. Paul, MN: West.

Giacopassi, D. (1987). Study of date rape. *Criminal Justice and Behavior, 14*, 175-193.

Glasser, M. (1988). Psychodynamics aspects of paedophilia. *Psychoanalytic Psychotherapy, 3*(2), 121-135.

Goldenson, R. (1970). *Encyclopedia of human behavior: Psychology, psychiatry and mental health.* Garden City, NY: Doubleday.

Goode, E. (1984). *Deviant behavior* (2nd ed.). Englewood Cliffs, NJ: Prentice-Hall.

Greenberg, J., Bruess, C., Mullen, K., & Sands, D. (1989a). Obscene phone callers. *Journal of Social Work and Human Sexuality, 11*(1), 15-25.

Greenberg, J., Bruess, C., Mullen, K., & Sands, D. (1989b). *Sexuality.* Dubuque, IA: Wm. C. Brown.

Groff, M., & Hubble, L. (1984). A comparison of father-daughter and stepfather-stepdaughter incest. *Criminal Justice and Behavior, 2*, 461-475.

Groth, A., & Burgess, A. (1977). Rape: A sexual deviation. *American Journal of Orthopsychiatry, 47*, 400-406.

Groth, A., Burgess, A., & Holstrom, L. (1977). Rape, power, anger and sexuality. *American Journal of Psychiatry, 134*, 1239-1243.

Groth, A., Longo, R., & McFadin, J. (1982). Undetected recidivism among rapists and child molesters. *Crime and Delinquency, 3*, 450-458.

Groth, N. (1979). *Men who rape: The psychology of the offender.* New York: Plenum.

Haas, L., & Haas, J. (1990). *Understanding sexuality.* Boston: Mosby.

Hagan, F. (1990). *Introduction to criminology* (2nd ed.). Chicago: Nelson-Hall.

Hall, D., Lawson, B., & Wilson, L. (1981). Command hallucinations and self-amputation of the penis and hand during a first psychotic break. *Journal of Clinical Psychiatry, 42*, 322-324.

Harrington, P. (1986). The disposition of father-daughter incestuous assault cases. *New England Law Review, 21*, 399-427.

Haydn-Smith, P., Marks, H., & Repper, D. (1989). Behavioral treatment of life-threatening masochistic asphyxiation: A case study. *British Journal of Psychiatry, 150*, 518-519.

Hazelwood, R., Dietz, P., & Burgess, A. (1983). *Autoerotic fatalities.* Lexington, MA: D. C. Heath.

Hazelwood, R., & Warren, J. (1989). The serial rapist: His characteristics and victims. *FBI Law Enforcement Bulletin, 58*(2), 18-25.

Heilbrun, A., & Seif, D. (1988). Erotic value of female distress in sexually explicit photographs. *Journal of Sex Research, 24*, 47-57.

Herman, J., & Hirschman, L. (1981). Families at risk for father-daughter incest. *American Journal of Psychiatry, 138*, 735-756.

Heston, L., & Shields, J. (1968). Homosexuality in twins. *Archives of General Psychiatry, 18*, 149-160.

Hirsch, M. (1986). Narcissism and partial lack of reality testing. *Child Abuse and Neglect, 10*, 547-549.

Holmes, R. (1972). *Sexual behavior: Homosexuality, prostitution and swinging.* Beverly Hills, CA: McCutcheon.

Holmes, R. (1983). *The sex offender and the criminal justice system.* Springfield, IL: Charles C Thomas.

Holmes, R. (1984, February). Children in pornography. *Police Chief*, pp. 42-43.

Holmes, R. (1985). [Report to the Exploited and Missing Child Unit, Louisville, KY]. Unpublished manuscript.

Holmes, R. (1989). *Profiling violent crimes: An investigative tool*. Newbury Park, CA: Sage.

Holmes, R., & De Burger, J. (1985). Profiles in terror: The serial murderer. *Federal Probation, 53*, 53-59.

Holmes, R., & De Burger, J. (1988). *Serial murder*. Newbury Park, CA: Sage.

Illinois Legislative Investigative Committee. (1980). *Sexual exploitation of children: Report to the Illinois General Assembly*. Chicago: Author.

Irwin, J. (1988). Donald Cressey and the sociology of the prison community. *Journal of Criminal Law and Criminology, 34*, 328-337.

Janik, A., & Chromy, K. (1979). A case of necrophilia. *Ceskoslovenske Psychiatrie, 75*, 305-306.

Jenks, R. (1985). Swinging: A test of two theories and a proposed new model. *Archives of Sexual Behavior, 14*, 517-527.

Kallman, F. (1952a). Comparative twin study in the genetic aspects of male homosexuality. *Journal of Nervous and Mental Disease, 115*, 283-298.

Kallman, F. (1952b). Twin and sibship study of overt male homosexuality. *American Journal of Human Genetics, 4*, 136-146.

Kant, H., & Goldstein, M. (1973). *Pornography and sexual deviance: A report of the legal and behavioral*. Berkeley: University of California Press.

Karpman, B. (1957). *The sexual offender and his offenses*. New York: Julian.

Katchadourian, H., & Lunde, D. (1975). *Fundamentals of human sexuality*. New York: Holt, Rinehart & Winston.

Kaufman, A. (1980). Male rape victims: Noninstitutionalized assault. *Journal of Psychology, 137*, 221-223.

Kinsey, A., Pomeroy, W., & Martin, C. (1948). *Sexual behavior in the human male*. Philadelphia: W. B. Saunders.

Knight, R., & Prentky, R. (1987). The developmental antecedents in adult adaptations of rapist subtypes. *Criminal Justice and Behavior, 14*, 403-426.

Knox, D. (1984). *Human sexuality: The search for understanding*. St. Paul, MN: West.

Knox, D., & Wilson, K. (1981). Dating behaviors of university students. *Family Relations, 30*, 83-86.

Koss, M., Gidycz, M., & Wisniewski, N. (1987). The scope of rape: Incidence and prevalence of sexual aggression and victimization in a national sample of higher education students. *Journal of Consulting and Clinical Psychology, 55*, 162-170.

Lahey, B. (1989). *Psychology: An introduction* (3rd ed.). Dubuque, IA: Wm. C. Brown.

Lancaster, N. (1978). Necrophilia, murder and high intelligence: A case report. *British Journal of Psychiatry, 132*, 605-608.

Lauder, R. (1985). *Fighting violent crimes in the United States*. New York: Dodd, Mead.

Lavrakas, P. (1981). On households. In D. Lewis (Ed.), *Reactions to crime*. Beverly Hills, CA: Sage.

Leising, P. (1985). The negative effects of the obscene telephone caller upon crisis intervention services. *Crisis Intervention, 14*, 84-92.

Lesee, S. (1984). Klismaphilia. *American Journal of Psychotherapy, 51*(5), 175-183.

Levine, E., & Kanin, E. (1987). Sexual violence among dates and acquaintances: Trends and their implications for marriage and family. *Journal of Family Violence, 2*, 89-98.

Linz, D. (1989). Exposure to sexually explicit materials and attitudes toward rape: A comparison of study results. *Journal of Sex Research, 26*, 50-84.

Lowenstein, L. (1989). The etiology, diagnosis and treatment of the fire-setting behavior of children. *Child Psychiatry and Human Development, 19*(3), 186-194.

Lowery, S., & Wetli, C. (1982). Sexual asphyxia: A neglected area of study. *Deviant Behavior, 4,* 19-39.

Luke, J. (1967). Asphyxial deaths by hanging in New York City. *Journal of Forensic Sciences, 12,* 359-369.

Lynn, B. (1986). *Polluting the censorship debate: A summary and critique of the final report of the Attorney General's Commission on Pornography.* Washington, DC: American Civil Liberties Union.

MacDonald, J. (1971). *Rape: Offenders and their victims.* Springfield, IL: Charles C Thomas.

MacNamara, D. (1965). Male prostitution in an American city: A pathological or socioeconomic phenomenon. *American Journal of Orthopsychiatry, 35,* 204.

Macy, J. (1979). To the reader. In Office of Planning and Evaluation, *Arson: The federal role in arson prevention and control* (report to the Congress). Washington, DC: Office of Planning and Evaluation.

Malamuth, N., & Donnerstein, E. (1982). The effects of aggression-pornographic mass media stimuli. *Advances in Experimental Psychology, 15,* 103-136.

Mano, K. (1985, February). The phone sex industry, part II. *National Review, 37,* 59-60.

Marmor, J. (1980). The multiple roots of homosexual behavior. In J. Marmor (Ed.), *Homosexual behavior: A modern reappraisal* (pp. 3-22). New York: Basic Books.

Marshall, L. (1988). The use of sexually explicit stimuli by rapists, child molesters, and non-offenders. *Journal of Sex Research, 25,* 267-288.

Masters, R., & Roberson, C. (1990). *Inside criminology.* Englewood Cliffs, NJ: Prentice-Hall.

Matek, O. (1988). Obscene phone callers. *Journal of Social Work and Human Sexuality, 11*(1), 15-25.

Mayerson, S., & Taylor, D. (1987). The effects of rape with pornography on women's attitudes and the mediating role of sex role stereotyping. *Sex Roles, 17,* 321-338.

McCarthy, K. (1984, June 10). Serial killers: Their deadly bent may be set in cradle [interview with H. Morrison]. *Los Angeles Times,* sec. 2, p. 6.

McCarthy, S. (1982). Pornography, rape and the cult of macho. In J. H. Skolnick & E. Currie (Eds.), *Crisis in American institutions* (pp. 218-232). Boston: Little, Brown.

McCarty, L. (1986). Mother-child incest: Characteristics of the offender. *Child Welfare, 65,* 447-457.

McCary, J. (1978). *McCary's human sexuality.* New York: D. Van Nostrand.

McIvor, D., & Guthrie, B. (1986). MMPI profiles of incest offenders: Men who molest younger children and men who molest older children. *Criminal Justice and Behavior, 13,* 450-452.

McKinnon, I. (1979). Child pornography. *FBI Law Enforcement Journal, 48*(2), 18-20.

McShane, C. (1988). *Warning: Dating may be hazardous to your health.* New York: Mother Courage.

Melella, J., Travin, S., & Cullen, K. (1989). Legal and ethical issues in the use of antiandrogens in treating sex offenders. *Bulletin of the American Academy of Psychiatry and Law, 17,* 223-231.

Mendelson, B. (1963). The origin and doctrine of victimology. *Excerpta Criminologica, 3,* 239-244.

Meyer-Bahlburg, H. (1977). Sex hormones and male homosexuality in comparative perspective. *Archives of Sexual Behavior, 6,* 297-325.

Michaud, S., & Aynesworth, H. (1983). *The only living witness.* New York: Linden.

Milner, R. (1981). Orgasm of death. *Hustler, 8,* 33-34.

Money, J. (1980). *Love and sickness.* Baltimore: Johns Hopkins University Press.

Money, J. (1984). Paraphilias: Phenomenology and classification. *American Journal of Psychotherapy, 38,* 164-179.

Money, J. (1985). *The destroying angel.* Buffalo, NY: Prometheus.

Money, J., & Musaph, H. (1977). *Handbook of sexology.* Amsterdam: Elsevier/North Holland.

Money, J., & Werlas, J. (1982). Paraphiliac sexuality and child abuse: The parents. *Journal of Sex and Marital Therapy, 8,* 57-64.

Murphy, N., & Fain, T. (1978, October 19). *Psychobiological factors in sex and gender identity.* Paper presented at the annual meeting of AASECT, Portland, OR.

Murray, F., & Beran, L. (1968). A survey of nuisance telephone calls received by males and females. *Psychological Record, 18*(1), 107-109.

Nadler, R. (1968). Approach to psychodynamics of obscene telephone calls. *New York State Journal of Medicine, 68,* 521-526.

Nanjundappa, G. (1987). Profiles of juvenile male incest perpetrators: Treatment implications. *Journal of Offender Counseling, 15,* 25-31.

Nawy, H. (1973). In pursuit of happiness: Consumers of erotica in San Francisco. *Journal of Social Issues, 29,* 147-161.

Nelton, S. (1987). Learning how to cry rape. *Nation's Business,* pp. 67-68.

Nobile, P., & Nadler, E. (1986). *United States of America vs. sex: How the Meese commission lied about pornography.* New York: Minotaur.

O'Brien, S., & Goldstein, S. (1988, Spring-Summer). Why did they do it: Stories of eight convicted child molesters. *Journal of Criminal Law and Criminology, 34.*

O'Grady, J. (1988, December 23). Mother knows best. *New Statesman Society, 1,* 29.

Oliver, J. (1974). *Clinical sexuality.* Philadelphia: J. B. Lippincott.

Orlando, J., & Koss, M. (1983). The effect of sexual victimization on sexual satisfaction: A study of the negative-association hypothesis. *Journal of Abnormal Psychology, 92*(1), 104-106.

Oules, J., Boscredon, J., & Bataille, J. (1977). A case of gerontophilia. *Evolution Psychiatrique, 42,* 243-257.

Padgett, V., & Brislin-Slutz, J. (1989). Pornography, erotica, and attitudes toward women: The effects of repeated exposure. *Journal of Sex Research, 26,* 479-491.

Parker, G. (1987). An exploration of bestiality as a crime. *Criminal Justice Abstracts, 19,* 663-671.

Parrot, A. (1989). Acquaintance rape among adolescents: Identifying risk groups and intervention strategies. *Journal of Social Work and Human Sexuality, 12*(4), 21-39.

Petersen, J., Kretchmer, A., Nellis, B., Lever, J., & Hertz, R. (1983, January). The *Playboy* readers' sex survey. *Playboy,* p. 108.

Pollack, N. (1988). Sexual assault of older women. *Annals of Sex Research, 1,* 523-532.

Polson, C., & Gee, D. (1973). *The essentials of forensic medicine* (3rd ed.). Oxford: Pergamon.

Pope, R. (1978). Child pornography: A new role for the obscenity doctrine. *University of Illinois Law Forum, 47,* 711-757.

Queen's Bench Foundation. (1976). *The rapist and his crime.* New York: John Wiley.

Rada, T. (1978). Alcoholism and forcible rape. *American Journal of Psychiatry, 32,* 444-446.

Ressler, R. (1986a). Murderers who rape and mutilate. *Journal of Interpersonal Violence, 1,* 273-287.

Ressler, R. (1986b). Sexual killers and their victims: Identifying patterns through crime scene analysis. *Journal of Interpersonal Violence, 1,* 288-308.

Ressler, R., Burgess, A., & Douglas, J. (1988). *Sexual homicide: Patterns and motives.* Lexington, MA: Lexington.

Revitch, E., & Schlesinger, L. (1989). *Sex murder and sex aggression: Phenomenology, psychopathology, psychodynamics and prognosis*. Springfield, IL: Charles C Thomas.

Ringwalt, C., Christopher, P., & Earp, J. (1988). Attributing responsibility in cases of father-daughter sexual abuse. *Child Abuse and Neglect, 12*, 273-281.

Rizzo, N. (1981). Can everyone be rehabilitated? *International Journal of Offender Therapy and Comparative Criminology, 25*(1), 40-46.

Rodenas, J., Osuna, E., & Luna, A. (1989). Alcohol and drug use by rapists and their victims. *Medicine and Law, 8*(2), 157-164.

Romero, J., & Williams, L. (1985). Recidivism among convicted sex offenders: A 10 year followup study. *Federal Probation, 49*(1), 58-64.

Rosenfield, A. (1985, April). Sex offenders: Men who molest, treating the deviant. *Psychology Today*, pp. 8-10.

Rosman, J., & Resnick, P. (1989). Sexual attraction to corpses: A psychiatric review of necrophilia. *Bulletin of the American Academy of Psychiatry and the Law, 17*(2), 153-163.

Russell, D. (1983). *Rape in marriage*. New York: Collier.

Sadock, B., Kaplan, H., & Freedman, A. (1976). *The sexual experience*. Baltimore: Williams & Wilkins.

Saghir, M., & Robins, E. (1973). *Male and female homosexuality: A comprehensive investigation*. Baltimore: Williams & Wilkins.

Salter, A. (1989). *Treating child sex offenders and their victims*. Newbury Park, CA: Sage.

Samaha, J. (1988). *Criminal justice*. St. Paul, MN: West.

Saunders, E. (1989). Life-threatening autoerotic behavior: A challenge for sex educators and therapists. *Journal of Sex Education and Therapy, 15*, 82-91.

Schultz, L. (1980). *Sexual victimology of youth*. Springfield, IL: Charles C Thomas.

Scott, J. (1988). Book reviews of Attorney General's Commission on Pornography and related works. *Journal of Criminal Law and Criminology, 78*, 1145-1165.

Sheehan, W., & Garfinkel, B. (1988). Adolescent autoerotic deaths. *Journal of the American Academy of Child and Adolescent Psychiatry, 27*, 367-370.

Sheley, J. (1979). *Understanding crime: Concepts, issues, decisions*. Belmont, CA: Wadsworth.

Shelp, E. (1987). *Sexuality and medicine* (Vol. 2). Dordrecht, Netherlands: Reidell.

Shuster, S. (1975). Jack the Ripper and the doctor identification. *International Journal of Psychiatry, 6*, 385-402.

Silva, J., Leong, G., & Weinstock, R. (1989). Infibulation. *Psychomatic, 30*(20), 228-230.

Sivaloganathan, S. (1984). Aqua-eroticum: A case of auto-erotic drowning. *Medical Science Law, 24*, 300-302.

Stack, A. (1983). *The lust killer*. New York: Signet.

Stets, J., & Pirog-Good, M. (1989). Patterns of physical and sexual abuse for men and women in dating relationships: A descriptive analysis. *Journal of Family Violence, 14*, 111-119.

Stoller, R. (1982). Erotic vomiting. *Archives of Sexual Behavior, 11*, 361-365.

Stoller, R. (1985). *Observing the erotic imagination*. New Haven, CT: Yale University Press.

Stoller, R. (1986). *Sexual excitement: Dynamics of erotic life*. New York: American Psychiatric Press.

Storms, M. (1978). Attitudes toward homosexuality and femininity in men. *Journal of Homosexuality, 3*, 257-363.

Sturup, G. (1968). Treatment of sexual offenders in Hertedester, Denmark. *Acta Psychiatricia Scandinavica, 44*, 1-45.

Tappan, P. (1971). Some myths about the sex offender. In M. Wolfgang & L. Radzinoiwicz (Eds.), *The criminal society*. New York: Basic Books.

Thomas, C. (1985). *Taber's cyclopedic medical dictionary*. Philadelphia: F. A. Davis.

Tingle, D., Bernard, G., Robbins, L., & Newman, G. (1986). Childhood and adolescent characteristics of pedophiles and rapists. *International Journal of Law and Psychiatry, 9*(1), 103-116.

Tjaden, P. (1988). Pornography and sex education. *Journal of Sex Research, 24*, 208-212.

Tourney, G. (1980). Hormones and homosexuality. In J. Marmor (Ed.), *Homosexual behavior*. New York: Basic Books.

Turner, R. (1988). Rape: The myths and realities. *Ebony, 43*, 108.

U.S. Department of Justice, Bureau of Justice Statistics. (1987). *Data report*. Washington, DC: Government Printing Office.

Vaughn, M., & Sapp, A. (1989). Less than utopian: Sex offender treatment in a milieu of power struggles, status positioning, and inmate manipulations in state correctional institutions. *Prison Journal, 69*(2), 73-89.

Vinogradov, S., Dishotsky, N., Doty, A., & Tinklenberg, J. (1988). Patterns of behavior in adolescent rape. *American Journal of Orthopsychiatry, 58*, 179-187.

Walker, S. (1988). *Sense and nonsense about crime*. Pacific Grove, CA: Brooks/Cole.

Wark, V. (1982). Working with the sex caller. *Crisis Intervention, 12*(1), 13-23.

Warshaw, R. (1988). *I never called it rape: The Ms. report on recognizing, fighting, and surviving date and acquaintance rape*. New York: Sarah Lazin.

Weeks, J. (1986). *Sexuality*. New York: Ellis Horwood.

Weir, S. (1987). Thrills on the line. *New Society, 81*, 17-18.

Welch, R. (1988). Treating sex offenders. *Corrections Compendium, 13*(5), 1-10.

Wells, L. (1981). Family pathology and father-daughter incest: Restricted psychopathy. *Journal of Clinical Psychiatry, 42*, 197-201.

Wilson, W. (1988). Rape as entertainment. *Psychological Reports, 62*, 607-610.

Wilson, W., & Abelson, H. (1973). Experience with and attitudes toward explicit sexual materials. *Journal of Social Issues, 29*, 19-39.

Wise, T. (1982). Urethral manipulation: An unusual paraphilia. *Journal of Sex and Marital Therapy, 8*, 222-227.

Wyatt, G. (1985). The sexual abuse of Afro-American and white-American women in childhood. *Child Abuse and Neglect, 9*, 507-519.

Index

About the Author

Ronald M. Holmes is Professor of Justice Administration at the University of Louisville, Kentucky. He lectures nationally on sex crimes and homicide investigations as well as on the investigation of ritualistic crimes. He is the author of *Profiling Violent Crimes: An Investigative Tool*; *The Sex Offender and the Criminal Justice System*; and *Sexual Behavior: Homosexuality, Prostitution and Swinging*; and coauthor (with James De Burger) of *Serial Murder*. He has authored articles that have appeared insuch national journals as *Federal Probation, The American Journal of Criminal Justice, Police Chief, Police Marksman, The Journal,* and the *New Eng-land Journal on Civil and Criminal Confinement*. He is also a deputy coroner in Kentucky and has assisted in the evaluation of sex-related homicides and suicides for police departments not only in Kentucky but across the United States.